Flying Wing

FLYING WING
AN AUTOBIOGRAPHY

Rory Underwood

with David Hands

Stanley Paul
London

Stanley Paul & Co. Ltd

An imprint of Random House (UK) Limited

20 Vauxhall Bridge Road, London SW1V 2SA

Random House Australia (Pty) Ltd
20 Alfred Street, Milsons Point, Sydney 2061

Random House New Zealand Limited
18 Poland Road, Glenfield, Auckland

Random House, South Africa (Pty) Ltd
PO Box 337, Bergvlei 2012, South Africa

First published 1992
Copyright © Rory Underwood 1992

Set in Sabon
by Deltatype Ltd, Ellesmere Port

Printed and bound in Great Britain by
Clays Ltd, St Ives PLC

A catalogue record for this book is available from the British Library

ISBN 0 09 175074 1

Contents

	Acknowledgement	vii
	Foreword by Geoff Cooke	ix
1	Leaving on a jet 'plane	1
2	From East to West	9
3	So this is rugby	18
4	Growing pains	26
5	*Per ardua ad astra*	33
6	'This may be a spoof but . . .'	48
7	Flying high – and low	67
8	World Cup woes	82
9	Cooke's new recipe	93
10	The year of the Lion	109
11	Grand slam	128
12	On top of the world – nearly	140
13	Back to back	156
14	Try and try again	165
	The last word by Rob Andrew	173
	Career record	175

To my father

James Ashley.

I wish you could have seen it all.

Acknowledgement

Many people have helped me along the way and I hope that, if they read this book, they will recognise how grateful I am. In particular the RAF has been a most understanding employer, allowing me the time to be an ambassador for them as well as for rugby. But in bringing the words to life I would like to thank Ian Robertson of the BBC, whose idea it was, and David Hands of *The Times*, with whom I met in a variety of places – from hotel rooms in Melbourne to the West Car Park at Twickenham – as we both tried to find the time to put the flesh on the bones of my career. Roddy Bloomfield, at Stanley Paul, has taken the gamble that the results will turn out well and I hope he feels they have.

To Tudor Thomas, team secretary at the Tigers, thanks for your patience. To the Tigers, what a family! And to all the England players I have played with, especially those in recent years. There are one or two bad memories but thousands of good ones – long may English rugby's resurgence continue.

I must make particular mention of Geoff Cooke and Rob Andrew for taking the time to pen the start and the finish of the book – Rob may feel it should be the other way round – and of Sir Michael Knight and Gerald Davies for offering their particular reflections on my career. Stephen Comer (Middlesbrough), Bob Barker and Tony Hopkins (Leicester) and Tony Simpson (Yorkshire) made invaluable contributions to the statistical appendix.

Two other people deserve the greatest appreciation. The first is Kevin Murphy, known to all rugby players for Lancashire, England and the British Lions as 'Smurf'. Kevin has been England's physiotherapist for more years than he cares to remember; he has been a friend and a constant source of humour on tour, as well as keeping my body in one piece. The second person – the best waits for last – is Wendy, my wife, who has supported me at all times. It is not easy for rugby wives now that so much time is demanded of their husbands by rugby, and it has been particularly difficult during the last two years since the birth of our two daughters, Rebecca and Alexandra; but the friendships we have both made will last long after I have finished playing.

There has been liberal use of nicknames throughout the book, which I hope will not baffle the reader. Such names abound in rugby, as in most sports, and it would seem unnatural for me not to refer to friends and playing colleagues in such a familiar, comfortable way. Thus JC refers to John Carleton, 'Slem' to Michael Slemen, both former England wings of distinction; most of the nicknames for recent England team members are self-explanatory, as in 'Webbie' for Jonathan Webb, 'Hallers' (Simon Halliday), 'Teaguie' (Mike Teague), 'Deano' (Dean Richards), 'Winters' (Peter Winterbottom), 'Skins' (Mickey Skinner) and so on.

Photographic acknowledgement

The author and publishers would like to thank the following for allowing them to use their copyright photographs: Russell Cheyne/ AllSport, Colorsport, RAF Valley, *The Times*, Bob Thomas Sports Photography, Mike Brett, Roger Parker, P. R. Foster, David Ashdown/*Independent*, Raymonds Press Agency, Eddie Keogh/ *Today*, Mark Baker/Reuters and Ted Blackbrow/*Daily Mail*.

Foreword

By Geoff Cooke, honorary England team manager since 1987

Not many sports performers, let alone rugby players, really justify the epithets often showered upon them in praise of their ability. There are, however, a special few whose sheer brilliance on occasions makes you catch your breath in wonder and, to some extent, in envy.

Rory Underwood is one of that rare breed of truly outstanding sportsmen whose performances will live long in the memory of those of us privileged to see him in action. When he announced his retirement from international rugby at the end of the 1992 Five Nations championship, Rory was at the height of his powers and had sealed his place in history as one of the great rugby union wingers of all time.

It has been a special privilege for me to have been closely associated with Rory's representative career, from the first of his 20 caps for Yorkshire in 1982, then via the Northern Division, to his 55 caps and 35 tries for England. I well remember a prop forward colleague on the Yorkshire selectors declaring that he had seen the best young wing three-quarter prospect in England playing for Middlesbrough and Durham County, and the buzz of excitement when we learned that the boy was qualified to play for Yorkshire.

Of all his many tries, one Rory scored for Yorkshire against Lancashire at Headingley on a Wednesday evening in the county championship stands out in my memory. He received the ball deep in his own half with defenders converging on him but he simply turned on the turbo-boost and scorched away from them up the left wing, beat the full-back with a wonderful combination of swerve and change of pace and cantered over for his try. I still remember the gasps of astonishment from the crowd around me and the misting of the eyes that comes with the realisation that you have just witnessed something very special.

When I was appointed England team manager I recall Tom McNab, the national fitness adviser, enthusing about Rory's athletic prowess. Tom is a former national athletics coach and, in a battery of tests he devised for the England team in 1987, Rory produced such outstanding results that Tom reckoned only Daley Thompson at his best could have matched him. Rory has been blessed with a wonderful combination of pace, power and skill which is not given to many, and he has used his gifts so well.

Although Rory scored only four tries for England in his first 22 international appearances, he went on to score 31 more in his next 33 games. He became the deadliest finisher in world rugby and a key component in England's renaissance as a rugby power, and the try he scored against Ireland at Lansdowne Road in 1991 — which gave England the triple crown and led them to the grand slam — was arguably the most important of all.

Games against Ireland have been very significant for Rory. He was not exactly thrilled when I suggested he move over to the right wing to accommodate Chris Oti in the match against Ireland in 1988, but in many respects that was a turning point in his career. Rory scored two tries in that match and I'm sure that this switch gave him more confidence in his own abilities as an all-round rugby player. Things did not always go according to plan, however, and I remember his despair when he blamed himself (needlessly) for the mistake that allowed Wales to score the crucial try at Cardiff which denied England the championship in 1989.

But underneath the quiet, unpretentious and laid-back exterior there has always been a core of inner steel in Rory Underwood which would show itself when the occasion demanded. His desire to win sharpened and became increasingly obvious in his last two seasons, and pride of place on the wall in my office is given to the photograph of Rory's exultant leap in celebration of the final whistle marking England's grand-slam triumph over France at Twickenham in 1991. His contributions in team discussions, while still understated, became more frequent and significant as his confidence and experience developed, and I have always been grateful for his thoughtful observations, invariably offered with great diffidence.

Rory has never sought or cultivated the limelight, yet in his own unassuming way he earned the total respect and admiration of his team colleagues and his many opponents and became an idol for thousands of youngsters. What parents could wish for a better role model for their son?

Geoff Cooke
Leeds, April 1992

1

Leaving on a jet 'plane

On 7 March 1992 twenty-one England rugby players mounted the steps in front of Twickenham's committee box and waved contentedly to the crowd which had gathered below to cheer a second successive grand slam. None of those players had known such an occasion; few of those watching could remember the last time that one of the competitors in the Five Nations championship, fought out annually between England, Scotland, Ireland, Wales and France, had achieved victories against the other four two years running.

Few, indeed, could remember such a season, probably because there had never been one like it in the game's history; it was the season in which rugby union, through the second World Cup tournament, became public property and so, by extension, did its leading exponents. In the 1991–92 Rothmans Rugby Union Yearbook Rory Underwood was described as 'the most lethal finisher in the world, bar none'. Only Gerald Davies, the great Welsh wing of the 1970s, 'could match Underwood in the ability to squeeze in for tries under the noses of the cover defence, that final sinew-straining dive which is bound to end in pain and tackles', the yearbook claimed. So was this the time to go, to leave it all when the game's profile had never been higher and when the amateur regulations, for the first time, permitted players to capitalise financially on their fame?

In Rory's mind there was little doubt. After eight years of international rugby, after a record-breaking number of games and tries for England, the equations no longer balanced. At 28 he was at the peak of his rugby-playing ability. The flowering of England over the previous three years had meant the blossoming of the Leicester wing, but for Rory, rugby has only ever been one side of his life – the other primary strands have been his family and his career in the Royal Air Force. Both required more time than rugby now allows – it was time to go.

His family, the RAF authorities, his playing colleagues, the England *team management, all knew of his decision. It had been hinted at strongly in various newspapers during the previous few months and that very morning, when England were to play Wales at Twickenham for the 1992 championship, The Sun had run an exclusive story to tell its readers why Rory had decided to leave international rugby. That too, was a commercial decision; very few players are starry-eyed about the amateur tradition of rugby union and, since the regulations now permitted him to do so, Rory and his advisers assessed the market for his retirement story and acted accordingly. Even so it is unlikely that many of the 60,000 who watched England's 24–0 win against the Welsh knew the curtain was coming down on a distinguished sporting career.*

I had always promised myself that I would choose the time to retire, the time that was right for me and the family. The process started as far back as the 1989 British Lions tour to Australia, at which stage the 1991 World Cup seemed an obvious target; I talked about it with Wendy, my wife, but that was all. I knew what my likely service commitments would be around that time, and that if I was to achieve my ambition to fly fast jets, that was when the opportunity would arise.

It's very easy for people to see only the sportsman, and from that point of view there was no obvious reason to retire. And I could have stayed at RAF Wyton, where I was based in a Canberra squadron, and continued to play rugby. But I was no longer enjoying the drudgery of training, the relentless travel to and from London – in the ten weeks covering the first training get-together of 1992 and the conclusion of the championship we had only one weekend off. Very few people realise the intense commitment that preparation for the game demands. If I was not with England I was with Leicester, going on their Pilkington Cup campaign to Fylde, to Waterloo, to Newcastle.

The game itself is not the problem. I still enjoy the pleasurable anticipation of arriving at the changing room, getting the kit on and playing a game of rugby. But the interval between the end of the World Cup in November and resuming club rugby confirmed in my mind that I had made the right decision. I took a fortnight off after the World Cup final against Australia and then, one wet Monday night, climbed into the car to drive to Leicester to train when I realised that I didn't want to go. 'I can do without this,' I thought, and it was not until I played my first game a week later, against Wasps, which went well, that some sort of appetite returned.

What I will miss most is being out on the stage, before a 60,000 crowd, performing. The other void will be the camaraderie, the squad spirit which was established, particularly within the group of players who represented England during my last three years. The contrast for me, and for other long-serving players like Peter Winterbottom, Wade Dooley, Rob Andrew, to what being part of the England team meant at the start of our careers is enormous. I can truthfully say that being with the recent squad has been like being with a family; there has been no animosity, no unhealthy rivalry. The attitude has been professional yet it has been tremendous fun.

Now, when I know the boys are preparing for another game and I'm not there, I will miss it: the familiar routine, meeting at the Petersham Hotel in Richmond on a Wednesday night, the late meal, the exchange of news as people come in; the Thursday morning training, dashing round to golf or whatever in the afternoon, the team meeting in the evening; the Friday session, probably going to the cinema in the evening, the leg-pulling, the nervous jokes on the Saturday of the game itself, the closing-in from the outside world.

Otherwise there will be few regrets. I would have enjoyed the chance of playing against South Africa, so inevitably people will say, 'Well, you should have hung on until November 1992.' But that adds another year because if you keep in trim for half the season you may as well complete it, and in any case I had made up my mind before it became known definitely that the South Africans would be back in international sport, let alone playing rugby in England. It would have been fun to have played in a full international with Tony, my brother, who has come so close to winning a cap and is, like me, a wing – though fortunately he plays on the right while I have spent most of my career as a left wing. The best we could manage was an appearance at Twickenham in 1990 in the same England XV that played the Barbarians in their centenary match. I have no doubt that he has it in him to play international rugby and to make up for the disappointment of touring with the senior side in Argentina in 1990 and missing the chance of a cap. He has the pace, he can beat people and he's not frightened to go for the corner – when I think of what I was like at his age I have absolute confidence in his ability to win caps.

I would like to have scored in all four games of a championship; twice, in 1990 and 1992, I came close but just missed. I wish Geoff Cooke had been team manager when my career started, rather than at the other end, because the standard of England rugby has soared since he joined us in 1987 – I would probably have scored 70 tries rather than 35.

Rugby has become a public commodity during that time. In a recent conversation Gary Lineker, the Tottenham and England footballer, said how much he noticed an increase in his personal profile after he won the Golden Boot for scoring the most goals of the 1986 football World Cup; the same has happened in rugby and we get recognised everywhere we go. It's a nice feeling. One weekend, just after ITV had made me the subject of *This Is Your Life*, I was stopped four or five times out shopping in Grantham market and congratulated on the rugby, on my children. When you sense the amount of enjoyment people derive from something in which you have been concerned, you can't help but get pleasure from it.

A successful England side in any sport engenders that kind of enthusiasm and the public recognition has brought unexpected honours which, for me, capped a marvellous concluding international season. The family returned home from a week's holiday in the West Country in mid-May to find a letter waiting from the Prime Minister's secretary to say that I had been recommended for an MBE in the Queen's 1992 Birthday Honours list. Words cannot say how proud I am to accept such an honour, at the end of eight years of international rugby; when you are training alone, or preparing as a team, or fending off the brickbats or accepting the praise, you never think about official recognition of this kind but it means a lot, to me as an individual, to my family and to the game.

I hope that I can continue to turn out on a regular basis for Leicester in the coming seasons, but that will depend upon the RAF and future postings because this year has been my chance to rejoin the fast-jet stream and fulfil my ambition to fly single-seat fighters. After the 1992 international season ended I returned to old haunts at RAF Valley on Anglesey to renew acquaintance with the Hawk, and by the time this book is published I hope to be going on to a tactical weapons unit at either Chivenor or Valley before selection for one of the front-line aircraft – Harrier, Tornado F3 or GR1, and Jaguar.

That will take immense concentration and will serve as a reminder that, had I been more successful in the early part of my flying career, I would certainly not have been in a position to play 55 times for England. The distribution of time between the RAF and my family will leave little enough for leisure pursuits but I would love to try to improve my golf and to accept some invitations to play in pro-celebrity tournaments, though they do tend to clash with my service commitments. I have played sport since school – swimming, tennis, squash – and I have no intention of turning into a slob, even though my diet may leave something to be desired. Dusty Hare told the world on *This Is Your Life* of my enjoyment of chocolate cake; Wendy, my wife, will tell you that vegetables and fruit do not feature to any great degree at meal-times.

And what of the game? So much has changed since I started playing, and the World Cup last year catapulted rugby union into the public eye as never before. The leading players now have, or have access to, the personal managers who are such a feature of professional sport. Who would have dreamed of that scenario as little as four years ago? Sport has demanded a great deal from the players, and changes to the game's amateur regulations mean that they can now gain some recompense away from the field of play.

The England squad over the last eighteen months has tried to develop that commercial area, in concert with several of the Rugby Football Union's leading administrators, but it's fair to say that many members of the RFU committee have not favoured the players' plans. There is nothing wrong with the game of rugby union itself but if fundamental change is required, it may be to the Union itself, which is still based on the counties. It is the counties, the constituent bodies as they are called, which administrate the game at local level, and do it well, but whose influence is disproportionate to their current playing standards.

In my view divisional rugby is the way forward, making as it does greater demands upon playing skills, but at the moment the four divisions, in the North, Midlands, London and South-West of England, have little money of their own and lack the independence they should have – unlike the major provinces of the southern-hemisphere countries of Australia, New Zealand and South Africa.

The divisions are represented on the RFU committee only via the counties, rather than in their own right, and while there are a lot of good people on that committee there are also a lot of time-servers, people on the old-school-tie network who reach positions of influence because of whom they know and because they have the time, which more able types often have not. There are too many who are doing nothing, in my view, to help the modern game; it was welcome news that Paul Ackford, an outstanding second-row forward over the last four years, has agreed to represent Surrey on the RFU committee after the 1992 annual meeting, but he is only one voice in 56.

The gulf between what is required at county level, as a player or an administrator, and what is required at national level is far too wide for many people to bridge. Because some of the things that happen now did not happen in their day, they appear always to be putting a brake on progress rather than understanding what is necessary to compete at international level today, by talking to players, by talking to leading administrators from other countries so that they understand conditions as they are elsewhere – they don't have to agree with them but they need to know of the forces at work overseas.

Progress on the playing side of the game has been held up because of a lack of support for the divisional competition since it really got under way as a regular tournament seven years ago. I played county rugby for six years, with Durham but mainly with Yorkshire, and thoroughly enjoyed it. It acted as a springboard for me, but the county game did that for only a few; if you remove the best part of 100 players, the cream of the country, and put them into the divisional tournament, then scope is left for others below to show their worth for their counties.

But everyone in English rugby seems to want their slice of the action, their share of control rather than accepting a structure which feeds players through a system and acknowledges that, to improve, players will have to move – if they are seen playing well in county rugby a senior club is likely to express an interest. Then, if they are good enough, the divisional selectors will take them out of the club scene and so they will come to the attention of the England selectors. I think now the battle has been won, but still the counties as a whole are not happy and the same debates are held over and over again.

There is a place and a need for county rugby but not the one that used to exist. The league structure for clubs needs refining too, as seems likely to happen in 1993. My belief is that a nine-club division, playing 16 league games a season, would be ideal but it seems likely that ten-club divisions will become the norm. Sixteen league games, three divisional matches, four internationals, five cup matches at the most and a couple of spare Saturdays would give you 30 games and that's about right in a season. Ideally the Five Nations championship should start later in the year, so that it becomes the natural climax to the season.

The RAF has been fortunate to have two excellent representatives on the committee in Sir Michael Knight and Sir Michael Stear, and Peter Larter, a former England lock who replaced Sir Michael Knight this year, will also be good value. There are other like-minded committee men but too few in such a large committee. I understand that many of them are frightened of finding a professional game on their hands but the way to control it is not to say 'no' to everything but to take the bull by the horns and control it, find a way forward suitable both to those who play the game and to those who watch it in the future – not turning back to the past.

I don't think the money exists to support a professional game, though the exception is at international level – if a sponsor wanted to promote the Five Nations championship, for example. But I have never wanted to be paid for playing rugby union and, as far as I am aware, no member of the England squad does either. I see nothing wrong, though, in leaving the actual playing conditions as they are but permitting players to earn what they can away from the field of play. We all know the commercial opportunities that exist in the 1990s for sportsmen and women and the point is now that rugby union, like it or not, has reached a position where it is a commodity, where there is a demand for a good product and for the leading practitioners. The answer is for rugby union to use that situation to its advantage: to take the money that sponsors are willing to give for the good of the whole game and to construct a set of rules which will allow players to maximise whatever earning potential off the field they are considered to have. An advanced version of the England squad's Run with the Ball campaign, which has been approved by the International Rugby Football Board, is required and players would be very happy with that.

At the moment, in my opinion, the sponsors get a poor return for their money. Run with the Ball gave those companies who supported it the chance to have players available during the World Cup, when interest among youngsters was at its height. They received exposure of their products via the kit the players wore, and through the interest the players took with the children, whereas under the more formal arrangements made between the union and its sponsors, so much seems essentially static. Rugby benefits from campaigns such as ours. Certainly the players hope to make a few thousand pounds from personal appearances but the goodwill returned to the game is incalculable – not to mention the more tangible financial benefit for youth development – a fact which the RFU, through its own development officers, acknowledges.

As an individual I now have an agent and have been able to involve myself in one or two comparatively small sponsorship deals but, as always, the time available for such things as public relations activities is strictly limited, particularly for those of us who live well away from London. But there is a small trickle of money coming into the family bank account which is welcome for as long as it lasts – which depends how long I, or any other player who stops playing on the big stage,

remain in the public eye. Other players have found ways of doing so –
Bill Beaumont is a prime example, by the way he has applied himself to
being a successful team captain on the BBC's quiz programme *A
Question of Sport*; Jamie Salmon has done so through a weekly
column in the *Daily Telegraph*. The opportunities exist and I am sure
the RAF would have no objection to a limited arrangement such as
that, because they receive publicity from it too. That, though, is
something which you might say is up in the air at the moment!

2

From East to West

The year of Rory Underwood's birth, 1963, was significant for a variety of reasons: many people remember it as the year when John F. Kennedy, the young and charismatic President of the USA, was assassinated in Dallas. In Britain, Harold Wilson was elected leader of the Labour Party which was poised to become the party of government as the Conservatives wrangled among themselves following the resignation as prime minister of Harold Macmillan.

It was the year of the great train robbery, when the Glasgow to London mail train was robbed of £2.5 million and the material was provided for a film of the mid 1980s starring the rock musician Phil Collins. It was the year when the Russians sent a woman into space and the French sent a cat – both returned safely. More pertinently as far as the Underwood family was concerned, the new state of Malaysia came into being on 16 September, combining Malaya, Singapore, North Borneo and Sarawak: 24 hours later the new country broke off diplomatic relations with Indonesia.

If it was hot, climatically and politically, in the Far East it had been chilly indeed in Britain at the start of the year. The winter of 1962–63 brought freezing temperatures across Europe, the like of which had been unknown for decades. England suffered its worst snowstorms for 80 years and for the best part of three months frost wrapped its icy tentacles around the country, bringing sporting fixtures to a virtual standstill. However, the year was to burn its way into the perceptions of rugby union enthusiasts over the coming seasons because of the international which took place at Cardiff Arms Park on 19 January 1963: England beat Wales 13–6, which was not in itself remarkable but became so as the years passed and successive England XVs found themselves unable to repeat the feat. In fact it was another 28 years before England won again in Cardiff, when Rory was part of the team.

What was remarkable was that the match took place at all, since Cardiff was frostbound and even the copious use of straw to protect *the surface had little effect. Richard Sharp's England players had to prepare on the beach at Porthcawl when they gathered for the game, for fear of injury on the usual playing surfaces, but their seven newcomers proved far from overawed by the occasion and, amid the rattle of studs on the frozen soil, scored two tries to Wales's one with Sharp adding the conversions and a dropped goal for good measure. It presaged championship honours, for England were unbeaten that year, but Ireland denied them both the grand slam and the triple crown by forcing a scoreless draw in Dublin. It was, as it happened, England's last outright championship until the grand slam of 1980.*

All of which was of little interest in far-off Malaya where, the year before, James Ashley Underwood and Annie Tan had celebrated their wedding. 'Ash' Underwood, a native of Middlesbrough, was an engineering officer in the Merchant Navy before joining the sales staff of Harrisons Lister Engineering, a company whose head office was in London but with considerable interests in the Far East. His bride, the oldest of eight children, came from a family of Chinese–Malayan origins and they met when Annie, a shorthand typist, also joined Harrisons Lister and was invited to help Ash in his social duties to the company.

Home became 2 Chateau Garden in Ipoh, a mining town some 100 miles to the north of Kuala Lumpur on the Malayan peninsula. The predominant interests for the large expatriate population, many of them of Scottish or Irish extraction, were tin mining or rubber plantations and there was an active sporting and social life for adults and children. Ash Underwood, an enthusiastic footballer, helped teach the game to the local children in his spare time, while Annie had been no mean sprinter – a virtue apparent at a very early stage in her oldest offspring. It is no coincidence that the first school report for physical training for the five-year-old Rory from Tenby School in Ipoh reads: 'Very good. Doesn't know when to stop though!'

Rory was born on 19 June 1963, but not in Malaya. Annie Underwood, requiring treatment to a thyroid gland, had made the long trip to Middlesbrough (where she met her in-laws for the first time) and gave birth by caesarean section at the General Hospital to the first of her four children. The other three, Gary, Tony and Wendy, were all born overseas, the boys in Ipoh in 1964 and 1969 respectively and Wendy in Petaling Jaya in 1971. Rory's christening took place at the Church of the Holy Trinity in North Ormesby a month after his birth (in what was, rather appropriately, the Chinese year of the rabbit) and Ash Underwood, whose own father had also been named

James, had determined to break the family tradition: he was an enthusiastic cinema-goer and a popular star of the time was Rory Calhoun – which also offered a name which could not easily be shortened, although Rory's England colleagues subsequently managed it, if 'Rors' can be regarded as an abbreviation of any substance.

It was two months before my father laid eyes on me because he had returned to Ipoh before I was born. But my earliest memories are of the bungalow in Ipoh – it was set in an acre of ground and seemed huge to me, plenty of room to run and fight and play games. Because Gary was born only 17 months later and because we both went away to school in England at the same time, we were pretty close and got up to the usual pranks small boys do.

The one I remember was the adventure with a packing crate which my mother always tells people about. It was kept round the side of the house and had a tar lining to make it waterproof. We could creep into this crate but on this occasion I had found a box of matches and decided for some reason it would be a good idea to set light to it. I was only six or seven and I thought I would be able to put the fire out easily from the water basin nearby, but soon found that I couldn't. So I ran round the other side of the house and hid up a tree in the corner while the crate smouldered away. I don't think my parents were amused and I had to be dragged down from the tree to take my punishment.

A scar on the bridge of my nose is another relic from childhood. That happened when my parents had gone out for the evening and Gary and I, as we usually did in their absence, crept into their double bed. We ended up fighting in the dark and I hit my head on the corner of the bed, with visible effects; another time I was hit in the eye by a stone flung up from the lawnmower, but by and large it was a lovely life for children. We could go hunting for butterflies and I remember seeing the odd grass snake about the bungalow – though never anything worse.

I suppose it was a privileged kind of upbringing. We were Eurasians, we had Chinese servants – a cook named Ah Wee and his wife, Ah Eng, who was the amah who looked after us. It was not quite as posh as it sounds; that was the norm for people who had the sort of job my father did. I wasn't aware of any class distinctions, but then as a small child you are not. I was brought up speaking English – my father had neither Malay nor Chinese – and it would have been the perfect time to learn another language. Now I look back and regret that I didn't. I learned the odd word, basic numbers and polite expressions, but it was a wasted opportunity. My mother provided the discipline at home but it was a free and easy existence and I suppose, looking back, we were pretty pampered. Nevertheless I don't think we ever went around thinking we were the bees' knees, either in Malaysia or when we were in England; we were brought up to be polite and well-mannered, though you must remember that in Malaysia the ethical approach is that if you don't work, you don't earn. There's no such thing as the welfare state; but the Asian mentality is to work hard, to put money by, and it always irritates me when I hear people grumbling about what they feel they deserve the right to.

Perhaps that background helped make me a fairly open-minded person. I wasn't a very patient child and sometimes I would get bored very easily. It took me a long time to get into the habit of reading books; I would have the odd hobby but nothing stuck and generally we, as children, depended on each other for our activities. Now I realise how lucky I was in my upbringing and I hope the sense of proportion I have been able to develop from what may be regarded as an unusual background can be passed on to my own family.

My first school was the Rowley Kindergarten in Ipoh, where I began in 1966 when I was nearly three. Two years later I started as a day boy at Tenby, also in Ipoh, but I was only there for 15 months because in 1969 the family moved to Kuala Lumpur – there was quite a lot of tension between Malays and Chinese in Malaysia at the time – and I had three months at Berwick Hills School in Middlesbrough as a stopgap before beginning at the Alice Smith School in KL. It was fairly formal schooling, based largely on the European style, and sport played a considerable part in it. Added to which Dad played football for the Selangor Club in KL, the club where the expatriates tended to go, which they nicknamed the 'Spotted Dog'! The padang out in front of the club had all the traditional team pitches – soccer, rugby, hockey, cricket – and the main bar inside was men only (it still was the last time I went there).

School reports in Malaysia were the usual mixture – 'Far too boisterous in class' the form mistress at Tenby wrote in one, 'easily distracted' appeared in another – but the PE reports were consistently good. When I got to Alice Smith the staff seemed to think I was a bit of a dreamer; I didn't always finish what I started. Maybe the changes in schools and in our home had something to do with that.

But the major change came in 1971. The usual choice for expatriates in Malaysia at that time was to send their children either to Australia or back to Britain for schooling and in my case the choice was dictated by my father's Yorkshire background. His parents were still in Middlesbrough and it was natural for him to look to that area; so that Christmas, when I was eight and Gary was seven, Dad took advantage of a long leave to take us to England, to a Parents' National Education Union school called Brignall Grange just outside Barnard Castle, a market town right on the southern edge of Durham's boundary with Yorkshire. This was our intermediate step before we went on to the Barnard Castle preparatory school and we spent two terms at Brignall; my reports for physical training ran 'Very good, shows promise' for the first term and 'excellent sense of movement' for the second. You can almost see the direction in which I was heading!

I don't remember it as a big wrench, leaving Kuala Lumpur, saying goodbye to my parents. I dare say we bawled our eyes out at the time but after that Gary and I just got on with adjusting to our new surroundings. I suppose we had become accustomed to the concept of travel by then and if we had not, we certainly did over the next few years, since we flew back to Malaysia each holiday. That didn't arouse much comment from classmates, although there would be the odd remark when we came back from holiday with the deepest of tans. Our grandparents lived a couple of hours away, at Middlesbrough, and it was my grandmother who put us on the bus to make the trip to Brignall first of all. But we were confused about the directions and, instead of hopping off the bus as it passed the school, we jumped out earlier at a pub called the Morrit Arms, which is about three miles from the school, where we thought we would be met. The headmaster therefore found himself short of two young Underwoods. So much for day one.

At that time Gary and I were of similar size and similar looks, so I suppose we stood out a bit as being 'different' to the other lads. Not that there were any what you might call racial vibes at Brignall, but when we got to Barnard Castle we did get teased a bit; it wasn't hostile, merely the sort of schoolboyish nicknames – Ping and Pong in our case! One of the great things about sport, though, is that it mixes everyone up and you come to accept people very easily for what they are or can do rather than the way they look. Both of us were reasonably good sportsmen and it helped. At the Alice Smith school I had won cups for sprints and I had played a lot of football; twice a week Dad had helped organise games and I played mainly on the wing even then. Curiously I remember more about the football than the sports days in Malaysia, because when school was over a gang of us would play on the front lawn of our bungalow, or Gary and I would play against each other.

It was football at Barnard Castle prep too. The town itself is an attractive place with, as the name suggests, a castle which dates back to the twelfth century. But both the main school and the prep school are out of the centre, on the east side of the town next door to the famous Bowes Museum. The houses at school are named after famous explorers and I was in Raleigh House for the two years I was there before I took the common entrance examination and moved up to the main school. Academically I suppose I was average – the standard 'could do better' pupil! I have never managed to overcome the difficulty my reports suggest I had when grappling with poetry, but invariably there seems to have been some complimentary remark about games. I don't think I was academically outstanding at any time in my career but I merely became part of the sausage factory, passed the required examinations and moved on, though, having a June birthday, I was young for my year.

I enjoyed school but mainly for the sport. 'A greater degree of organisation is obviously necessary in his work,' my tutor in York House wrote on my first report in the main school. 'However on the rugby field he is already quite a star performer with an amazing turn of speed.' Rugby was the game now; football had been left behind, something we didn't play seriously except if we had a bit of spare time. It was my first contact with rugby, which we played on Tuesday and Thursday afternoons. Someone handed a piece of paper round to ask the new boys if they had played before and, if so, in what position. I knew nothing about the game; I didn't read the papers at school and when I was at home it was back in Malaysia anyway. For me it was just another ball game. I said I was a wing, having played that position at football but not really knowing you had to be that quick to play there. We had no school matches at that early stage but I had the company of another promising games player because Rob Andrew started the same term, in the same house – we have stayed in touch ever since.

Rob very quickly moved into the fly-half position and he was captain in nearly every year as we moved up the school. He was an outstanding all-rounder – cricket, cross country and squash as well as rugby. I had only the three main sports, rugby, swimming and cricket. It was at school that I was dropped from a team for the only time I can remember. I played full-back once, the only time I moved away from the wing until the RAF played me at full-back in the inter-services championship at the end of the 1991 season. I made the first XV when I reached the lower sixth and we played a decent circuit, against schools like Pocklington, St Bees and Dame Allan's, though I can remember times when I would quite cheerfully have exchanged an English winter for the warmth of KL. One match in particular, against St Peter's, York, I spent the afternoon standing on the wing – Rob was kicking the leather off the ball – with the wind blowing, sleet pouring down, and I thought 'What am I doing here?' I was freezing and all I could think of was the school tuck shop about 50 yards from the end of the pitch, which had a fire; as soon as the whistle went I moved quicker than I had all afternoon.

It was not long after I had moved up to the main school that the family left Kuala Lumpur. Malaysia was going through a period of change which involved moving their own people into positions previously occupied by Europeans, but my father was able to stay with Harrison Lister by taking a post in Singapore; however my mother moved to England and bought a bungalow in the Startforth area of Barnard Castle, just south of the River Tees, preparing for the time when we would all be living together there. The bungalow is called 'Annash', running together my parents' forenames, which works quite well because it has a Malaysian feel to it. It can't have been easy for Mum, leaving her home for the north of England with in-laws close at hand whom she hardly knew, but over the years they grew to have a good relationship; as she says, she's a very adaptable person.

For a period she joined Gary and me flying to and fro between England and Singapore. The enjoyment of flying was already firmly implanted; sometimes we would be taken up to the flight deck to see the pilot operating and I used to write to all the airlines asking for information. Enjoyment of things Eastern was well implanted too, particularly food. Unfortunately when you have been used to the genuine article you either have to spend a large amount of money or go to London to experience the same in Britain; most Chinese takeaways and Indian curry houses in the UK have been thoroughly westernised. By and large it's a case of being filled up with rice and a couple of lumps of meat and a sauce, whereas in Malaysia there is a huge variety on offer and you can help yourself to so many different kinds of food and experience different tastes. When I was young I didn't like curry or particularly hot foods but I was able to take advantage of the choice on offer.

Maybe the change in family circumstances created a certain unease in my school activities. I got on well with most of the staff but the end of the academic year in summer 1977 produced the comment: 'He seems to be a little less ebullient lately – perhaps just end-of-term weariness.' If that was the case it lasted into the autumn, but

circumstances improved in the new year as I wrestled my way towards
my GCE O-levels – and took up Spanish as an option. I don't think
there was much debate about the possibility of my going on to higher
education and if there was, it probably ended in summer 1979 when I
came up with two O-levels at the first attempt – maths and physics –
which was something of a disappointment for my parents. I subsequently added English language, geography and art, the five passes
required for consideration by the RAF.

I was already determined by then that I wanted a service career. It
had developed from those early experiences of being allowed into the
cockpit while the aircraft was at 30,000 feet; I wanted to know what it
was like on take-off and landing, and that became a major curiosity. In
my third year at main school I joined the Air Force side of the
Combined Cadet Force – there was only a choice of Army or Air Force,
stuck in the middle of the Pennines we didn't have a Naval side! Ken
King, the house master, was very keen on discipline and urged people
to join; of our year, only two boys didn't and one was Rob. I had to
wait until the fifth form before I went on my first camp, to RAF
Cosford, which gave me the chance to look round the station sections
and have my first flight, in a Chipmunk. I was full of apprehension,
even more so when the pilot threw in some gentle aerobatics, but my
enthusiasm grew as I became accustomed to it and by the time the
sortie ended I was hooked. The following year we went to
Waddington and I flew again, while my third camp took me to RAF
Wyton – little did I know that several years later I would be based
there.

Every Wednesday the CCF paid a visit to RAF Leeming but it always
clashed with sport and I never flew while I was at school, although I
did get the chance of a week's gliding course at Arbroath and went solo
three times. Each flight consisted of only a few minutes but it provided
me with a taste of what I wanted – the experience of taking off and
landing. I watched with enthusiasm the careers films we were shown at
school, one in particular featuring a day in the life of a Jaguar pilot –
only one in 200 applicants get to fly Jaguars. I loved seeing the aircraft
screaming through the valleys, flying low, and one of the remarks I
remember being made was, 'You can't loop the loop in a jumbo jet.' I
loved the thought of the free expression, of being able to fly without
the hindrance that piloting a commercial aircraft inevitably brings. To
put it in a nutshell, the RAF propaganda worked for me. I just wanted
to fly.

I carried on my A-level courses in the sixth form – maths, physics and geography – and I enjoyed the geography but the net result bore out some of the reports I received during 1980–81. 'Present standard of work is very close to the pass/fail borderline' was one somewhat gloomy opinion and unfortunately it turned out to be the latter. I was disappointed but that was offset by the fact that I was clear in my own mind what I wanted to do and already had the necessary academic qualifications. Aptitude tests had already been arranged, which involved response times, basic arithmetic (I could cope with that well enough, as opposed to the more advanced maths we had done at school), hand–eye co-ordination, mock-up of control systems, and I came out of that with excellent results. My score was enough for me to apply for pilot and, better than that, I also achieved a flying scholarship which means the RAF get sponsors who will pay for the first 30 hours of flying tuition. Only another five hours are required for a pilot's licence.

I did my 30 hours at Cambridge, flying around in Cessna 150s; they are a single-engined high-winged training aeroplane, and I and three others were the last group that summer. One of the group was Steve Henderson, also from Barnard Castle and keen to join the RAF; I finished earlier than Steve, managed my five extra hours and got my private pilot's licence before I got my driver's licence. My parents were very supportive over my choice of career; we were settled at Startforth by now and neither of them had any qualms about it. I think they knew I wasn't university material!

3

So this is rugby

The wheel has come full circle for Rory now, since he is one of several England players whose development is shown in the comic-strip posters the Rugby Football Union has produced to popularise rugby with the youngsters of the 1990s. It was not always so. There was nothing in his background to suggest the international sportsman he has become when he took up the game first at Barnard Castle School. Rugby did not run in the family, and he did not read about it in the papers or watch it on the television.

But in 1974, when he moved on from preparatory school, rugby was riding high in Britain. The 1971 British Lions had created great enthusiasm for the game because of their success in the international series against New Zealand, success founded upon backs of the quality of Gareth Edwards and Barry John, Mike Gibson and John Dawes, wings of the quality of Gerald Davies, David Duckham and John Bevan, and at full-back the inimitable J. P. R. Williams. They were followed in 1974 by the unbeaten Lions captained by Willie-John McBride, who took South Africa by storm and whose only blemish was the drawn game in the fourth international of the series. But that side achieved domination among the forwards with a pack including Roger Uttley, who played international rugby in the second row, at No 8 and on the blind-side flank. Thirteen years later Uttley became England's coach.

It was not, though, a time of any great distinction in English rugby. True, England achieved back-to-back away wins over South Africa (1972) and New Zealand (1973) but in 1974 they finished bottom of the Five Nations championship and the likes of Duckham languished on the wing. They collected their only match points towards the end of the season, by drawing with France in Paris and beating Wales at Twickenham; they included in their ranks two players whom Rory was to come to know well – Alan Old, the fly-half who helped a young generation of Yorkshire backs develop, and Dusty Hare, then

Nottingham's full-back but subsequently Rory's colleague at Leicester.

Many children play games at school without continuing when they leave and I suppose I could have been lost to rugby – but for Middlesbrough. I had not achieved much outside Barnard Castle and though I had the pleasure of scoring a record number of tries – 41 I think it was – in my final term my mind was set on a career with the RAF, not on playing rugby, until Middlesbrough suggested I try my hand with them.

I went through school demonstrating no obvious strength of character. I was generally happy to fall in with whatever other people suggested and when it came to rugby, frankly, I was a bit of a coward. Tackling was not one of my fortes and in one practice, when I was 13, I was faced with quite a big lad against whom discretion seemed the better part of valour; however I screwed up my courage to make a tackle and, in doing so, collided with his knee, bruised my jaw and cut my lip, which didn't help create huge enthusiasm. It wasn't until the fifth form that I felt I had collected enough experience of the game to understand what I was supposed to be doing. But even though it was a bit of a slog at times I still enjoyed it – the fun of getting the ball and running with it, going off on the school bus to matches and missing a couple of lessons. I enjoyed the whole team ethic, in rugby, swimming or cricket, of trying to win. It was great to be part of the school's swimming team which came fourth in the intermediate age group of the national finals in Lincoln, but as I moved up the school there was less and less time for swimming.

None of us achieved any representative honours outside the school; Rob made Durham schoolboys under-15s team at cricket but I didn't come anywhere near to excelling until the sixth form. In my lower sixth year I made it on to the bench for the last Durham under-18 rugby match of the season and the following year I played for the team, as did Rob and three or four others from school. I did get an invitation to play in the North of England Schools trial, and scored a try for the junior XV, but I didn't play very well against boys who had far more experience and that was that. In that year John Goodwin, a colleague at England under-23 level later, played on the wing for the England under-18s and Barry Evans, whom I was to join at Leicester, played in the centre.

But there were so many other good rugby-playing schools in the north – Cowley were top dogs – and perhaps we couldn't get a look in.

I was content with the school season, when I managed to score six tries against Durham and 41 from our 15 games in all, which I think was a record. But John Oates, who was in charge of rugby, was the first to suggest that I might actually make the grade which, for someone as young and immature as I was then, was incomprehensible. I think he could see beyond the school's boundaries and recognise that I had certain natural abilities which could take me a long way in sport, but it just didn't mean anything to me at the time. All I wanted to do was enjoy myself.

But I had started to take an interest in rugby outside school. The year 1980 was that of England's grand slam and I can remember watching Dusty Hare put over the kick against Wales that won the match – and the equivalent fixture at Cardiff the following year when he missed the kick that would have won the match. I recall snippets but not a great deal; the grand slam as such didn't register.

I had no concept of club rugby but, as luck would have it, I didn't go straight from school into the RAF. Although I did quite well in the aptitude tests I think the selection panel recognised my immaturity during the interviews and discussion sessions and turned me down for a place on the next available course, which suddenly left a hole in my life to be filled. It did cause me some concern at the time but they had said, in effect, come back next year. So after I left school in the summer of 1981 I spent a vain few months doing retakes of my A-levels and then got a place on a Youth Opportunity Scheme, as an assistant to a local pewtersmith named Tom Neal. He was a nice guy and I really enjoyed myself; I was just helping out but I was allowed to make things, some of which went on sale, and it's something I would like to go back to as a hobby one day (if I can afford it).

By that stage I had already played for Middlesbrough. The initial contact came after John Oates arranged a game between the school and the club colts XV in Easter 1980. A little while later I took a phone call inviting me to play for Middlesbrough seconds and I was flabbergasted: this was a club whose name appeared in the results sequence on television and they wanted *me* to play for them. I couldn't believe it and was very excited.

It was at Sunderland and Dad drove me up there, as he had done to so many school matches after I became a day pupil. He must have been pleased that I was turning out for his town's rugby club, though he knew nothing about the game except what he picked up by watching it. He had not been able to watch me playing much at school but he was happy to drive me back and forth to Middlesbrough for training and games – it would have been about an hour there and an hour back

– until I got my driving licence. I played three games for the seconds and then made my first-team debut against Tynedale – I was still 16 (although the *Northern Echo* had me down as 17). My technique may have lacked something at that stage; my opposite number was considerably bigger than I was and my defensive method was to show him the outside then jump on him, which didn't prove tremendously effective, and Ian Wilkie quietly suggested that playing in this class of rugby it might be a good idea if I went for the legs instead. Ian was the Middlesbrough committee man who began the association between the club colts and school because his own son, Adam, went to 'Barnie'; obviously he wanted the association to continue!

At least I was starting to fill out by then. I used to be really weedy but I had got up to something like 12 stone and the extra weight came in handy. My game at that stage depended on sheer pace and teenage cheek, doing things which older wings might not have tried. I'm not sure my game has changed that much, it's the thinking behind it that changes. I haven't exactly got a sidestep though I can change direction quite well; I can cut back in and my main weapon is my swerve, but at that age you just go out and do what comes naturally. There were several of us from school who played for Middlesbrough during the 1980–81 season, friends like Rob, Richard Kent and Hugh Kelly.

We went our various ways during that summer but I resumed with Middlesbrough the next season, with the ambition of perhaps playing in the England colts team. During the close season I had been on a Rugby Football Union course at Rugby School for potential colts but I knew that the representative season did not begin until the new year so it was totally unexpected to receive the news from a friend, Steve Henderson, that the senior Durham side was interested in me. Steve had gone back to school for retakes of A-levels and I would pop in occasionally, to see old friends and to help with a bit of coaching, and it was he who, having read the papers more carefully than I, said, 'I see you're playing a county trial in a couple of weeks.'

I was more than surprised, but I turned up at Durham City, playing for the Rest, who went out and beat the prospective county XV 20–9, and I scored four tries. I couldn't go wrong and the following weekend I was named in the senior team to play the South of Scotland, the traditional Durham preparation for the county championship. The same night as I heard about that selection I received a telephone call from Dick Aspey, the Yorkshire team secretary, asking if I was interested in playing for his county – which was also the team of which Geoff Cooke was the chairman of selectors and Geoff, of course, was to have something of an influence on my career.

So there I was, this 18-year-old kid over the moon about being picked out for Durham, and Yorkshire wanting me too. At the same time there were one or two favourable comments appearing in the national newspapers. I had managed to score twice when Middlesbrough lost to Fylde and Billy Beaumont, then captain of England, was playing that day and seemed to think I had a future. I enjoyed that day at Fylde, it was a lovely playing surface and after the match Bernie Coyne, our hooker who played for Yorkshire, introduced me to Billy. He made some very kind remarks but I was thunderstruck about meeting international players (by the time I next met Billy, after the first county game, I had recovered sufficiently to go up and say 'hello').

But all my playing contacts were with Durham and there seemed a reasonable chance of playing through their championship season whereas Yorkshire was an unknown quantity, so I went with Durham who opened their campaign against Lancashire at West Hartlepool. All of a sudden, too, there was more than just the interest of the local papers; I can remember a radio interview one training night at Middlesbrough because the county opposition included Mike Slemen and John Carleton, then the current England wings (although JC had to withdraw with a broken collarbone). I was so nervous about it that I started gabbling about John Slemen and Mike Carleton – I could have bitten my tongue. As it happened I played opposite Nick Spaven from Sale and we were wiped out 44–9 with Spaven scoring four tries! There was more of the same in the next match, against Yorkshire, who played a three-quarter line all of whom had appeared, or would appear, for England – including Bryan Barley with whom I made my international debut. At least we kept the score of 23–4 to manageable proportions and I scored my first county try. Even better was the fixture with Cheshire, not only because we won but because I scored three tries – and managed to attract attention from Hull Kingston Rovers, the rugby league club.

I played out the championship season but after Christmas the colts season began and I knew, from the colts course at Rugby in the summer, that Durham would have a good side. Our first game, again, was with Lancashire, at Rochdale where the rain sluiced down and my opposite number was a player whom I came to know well – Nigel Heslop. We lost by a couple of points but won our remaining games to come second in the northern group and I was picked for the North of England trial against London, at St Mary's Hospital in London. We lost 16–15 in a morning game but then went to Twickenham to watch

England play Ireland, and what should the score have been but 16–15 – to Ireland. It was my first visit to Twickenham; two years later it was that fixture in which I made my international debut.

However, my ambitions at that stage were some way distant. I made my way via a trial at Birmingham to the England colts squad and secured a place in the side against France at Portsmouth – the first time my father saw me wearing England's international jersey. Several people were kind enough to write and congratulate me, among them Kenneth King from the Barnard Castle School staff who added a postscript advising me to 'steer clear of the after-shave lotion'. That was the season when England's senior squad had celebrated rather too well their victory in Paris and Colin Smart, the prop, had to be taken to hospital having drunk his gift bottle of after-shave under the impression it was wine. Maybe there are advantages to being teetotal.

I was playing opposite Eric Bonneval, whom France later used as both a centre and a wing at senior level, and that England side included Heslop (until he was replaced) and Mark Linnett, the Moseley prop who also went on to a senior cap. The French, though, had the better of us 16–3 and it's not a game of which I remember much – only that I played for England and I was so pleased and proud that several members of the family were there and could see me receive my cap at the ceremony during the after-match dinner.

That same weekend, after we returned home, my father died. The effects of such a blow to the family I deal with elsewhere. Sadly my grandfather, who was greatly affected by Dad's death, died scarcely a fortnight later, so to say that it was a difficult period for us all is merely stating the obvious. One element of good news at that time, for me anyway, came in the shape of an invitation to attend an England under-23 squad weekend – the only member of the colts side to be asked. So there was a lot of banter when we reassembled to play the Welsh Youth at Aberavon, a match we won 27–17 against a team including Adrian Hadley who, like me, was a left wing who went on to play for the full Welsh side before joining the exodus to rugby league of the late 1980s. We also rated five minutes on *Rugby Special*.

At that stage I was completely unaware that there was an under-23 tour in the offing, to Italy. I turned up, as required, to the squad meeting and won selection for the XV to play England Students at Sheffield in April 1982, though it was not a notable occasion: the students won 34–6 with a team including Simon Halliday, Mark Bailey – who played opposite me – and the big Bath full-back Chris Martin. Nevertheless the invitations did not stop coming; a week later

I was named in the tour party to play three matches in Italy that May along with several more who, nine years later, shared in England's grand slam and World Cup. Hallers was among the backs but the forwards included Brian Moore, Mike Teague and Gary Rees, with Stuart Barnes at fly-half.

So much rugby activity did serve to blunt any reflections about my father's death. Everything seemed to be happening at once; from playing a bit of schoolboy rugby to the senior county side and England under-23 was a major step in one season. The only way I could look at it then was that, at 18, I had another four years in which I might be able to tour with the under-23s. In my own mind I had made no connection with the senior England side — I was always one step behind, if you like. My ambition had been to play that season for Durham colts, and I played instead in the senior side; then I was playing for England colts, on top of the county matches.

At the same time I was being exposed to a glorious array of coaching standards and differing playing skills. At Middlesbrough, broadly speaking, we just went out and did it; playing for Durham seniors things began to change, with David Parker in charge, while England colts were looked after by Glenn Robertson, who had been a very good wing in his own playing days for Northampton and taught me some of the golden rules of wing play. Then Dick Greenwood, who later became England coach, took the under-23s; he was a great one for press-ups, as I recall, of which you can enjoy only so many.

Not that I was complaining. My only experience of touring had been a brief visit to Holland with a school party and though the under-23s were away for only eight days, I was looking forward to it. None of the others was overtly ambitious; we were all glad to be playing rugby abroad at someone else's expense. The different elements of the party soon came to the fore as we travelled by coach hither and thither in northern Italy — the four Gloucester lads, Teague, Steve Ashmead, Steve Baker and John Brain, always at the back of the bus. I went with no great opinion of myself as a rugby player; it was my habit then, and still is I suppose, to get on with whatever the next level required. It was instructive to see how others in my position prepared, players like John Goodwin, Roger Pellow and John Carr, but there was little enough time for the coaching of individual skills because we were so quickly into preparing for the first match, practising moves and so on.

It was a hard tour, three matches in eight days, and I played in them all. Dick proved a good motivator but the primary value for me was playing with and against different styles of players, learning just that bit more about myself and what I could do. By the end of it, though, I was feeling jaded, as were the half-dozen others who played all three games. We won the first two quite comfortably but in the 'international' – against the full Italian XV – I was opposite an older, more experienced player who got past me once or twice and I felt very heavy-legged. We lost 12–7 but I learned a lot, about touring, about getting on with other players; it was, in a sense, the climax to a year in which I had matured as a person in so many ways, being in the company of people many of whom were older than I was, spending more time away from home, travelling abroad. I felt I had 'survived' in higher company.

4

Growing pains

As a consequence of his Oriental background it would be easy to argue that Rory has a well-developed fatalistic streak in his make-up, though he prefers to describe himself as an 'optimist tinged with pessimism' — one who looks for the sunny side of life while accepting that the best laid plans can go awry. Certainly there is an adaptability in his character which he has inherited from his mother, who successfully overcame the major hurdle of moving from a comfortable existence in Malaysia to what would have been initially the entirely alien circumstances of life in Yorkshire.

At the same time both Rory and Gary acquired an independence born of their many school days spent traversing the globe, which stood both of them in good stead during the difficult days of 1981 when Ash Underwood died. 'Rory took all the responsibility when that happened,' Annie Underwood says. Perhaps, too, it was part of the maturing process which needed to occur before Rory began his career in the RAF, a process which the force's interview board may have recognised when the would-be pilot first came to their attention.

I'm a reasonably emotional sort of person — the kind perhaps who will let a tear fall at the end of a particularly sad film, for example — but I didn't cry the night my father died. A couple of years earlier I had been taken aback when I heard that John Wayne, the hero of so many Hollywood westerns, had died, and I still find it strange the way I accepted the passing of someone close to me. I'm sure the psychologists have the answer to it.

Sometimes when I look back I wonder at my reaction and whether it might have appeared callous. We had always enjoyed a comfortable relationship — not that chatty but we got on together, we always had done from the times when he had taught us football in Malaysia.

It's curious how I remember the last words I said to him, after our return home from the England colts' game with France at Portsmouth. We had stayed down south the Saturday night and made the long journey north on the Sunday, and before going to bed that evening I asked him to turn the sound down on the television. I was woken in the early hours of the morning by a neighbour who told me, without any preamble, that my father had died. He had been unwell for a while but he and my mother had kept from us how ill he was; he was only 54.

Looking back it's as though something clicked inside me, a response which said 'You have to sort this out, you have to look after your mother.' I walked out of one room and Mum was walking back from another; she was crying and I had to comfort her, and telephone my uncle who lived in Middlesbrough and just get through the rest of that night. At some stage I woke Gary up and in many ways his reaction was the same as mine, which I suppose you could describe as fatalistic. It's not that we didn't care but more an acceptance of what had happened and an acknowledgement of what needed to be done as a consequence.

On such an occasion there was no great awareness of being the oldest child, of becoming the head of the family, more a sense of trying to take care of the problems as they arose and in particular my mother, who was distraught. I don't recall subsequently any great feeling of emotion, even when I walked into my parents' bedroom the next day, where my father's body was lying, to fetch some clothes for Mum. I was aware of him lying beneath the sheet and I remember thinking, in some abstract way, that my father was under there but he was dead, inanimate; he was there but he was no longer there. If I put together any conscious thought, it was something along the lines of 'Why did he have to go?' Asking the question why he should have died when there should have been so much time left for him.

We had not spent much time together during the ten years before his death. He remained much of that time in the Far East and though Gary and I returned for holidays, he would still be at work and most of our time was spent with my mother. But in the couple of years before he died he was a great supporter; he would drive me everywhere, even to training; he would wait in the clubhouse while the players were outside, sharing a drink and chatting with any committee man who was there, and in the car afterwards he would ask questions about rugby, why this, that or the other happened. We didn't have the sort of relationship where we discussed life or emotional matters but we shared a friendship, we could crack a joke together. Maybe then he was not quite as well as I thought he was, which made him quieter than in those early days when we played football together.

He would have been so proud if he had been able to watch me doing well in my rugby career. He would have loved the visits to Twickenham, reading about games overseas in which I was playing, being able to meet the huge variety of people with whom rugby brings you into contact. That he did not do so has to be a huge regret. Even though he saw me playing for England colts he was never able to see me in a full international. The person who was worst affected by it, though, was my grandfather; obviously Mum was terribly distressed but my Grandad became very quiet and withdrawn after Dad died. It was as though he lost the will to live, he went downhill so quickly, and little more than a week later he died too.

I was fortunate that rugby provided me with a buffer, an outside interest that took me away from home and gave me something else to think about. At the time it was the colts with the under-23s hard on their heels; then, when a new season started, I was invited to play for Yorkshire. In between things started to move on the RAF front too. During the summer I had a letter concerning my application but pointing out that when I made my initial approach a medical test had shown that I had some slight calcification on one side of my nose, having damaged it a couple of years earlier playing rugby at school. In brief I was accepted pending an operation on the nose and I was told when I visited the Central Medical Establishment in London that I would have to have the earlier damage rectified.

That operation was organised for November 1982, which created a gap in the season for a period of convalescence. It was a season in which I moved from Durham to Yorkshire, which was a considerable wrench but I felt Yorkshire was the better side – they and Lancashire were the top two counties in the country. We had played some good rugby with Durham but won only two games. I wrote explaining my decision, that I was sorry to leave but that Yorkshire gave me the chance of going further in the game. It was a big decision to take. I talked to John Oates about it and it was valuable for me that he was there – not so much to make decisions for me but as a sounding-board, an older head who could point out the advantages and disadvantages. I spoke to some of the lads at Middlesbrough too, several of whom had played for Yorkshire, and the upshot was an appearance in a warm-up game against Calderdale. Two weeks later there was a further unexpected opportunity, to appear for the North against the touring Fijians; I was named as a replacement but when John Carleton withdrew injured, Mickey Harrison was called up – which was at least a right wing for a right wing. I drove up to Workington knowing I was rooming with Mickey – whom I had not met before – but it was not until I arrived that I discovered Mike Slemen had also pulled out, with influenza. That made the long journey to the north-west worth while, although I was happy enough just being involved with the division. The Fijians had done poorly in Scotland during the first half of their tour, and they again had little joy in England; the North welcomed them warmly then beat them 19–4 with Yorkshiremen getting all the points – two tries for me, one for Mickey and two conversions and a penalty for Alan Old. Every time I have played against the Fijians I have done well – in three internationals I have scored eight tries.

That was my introduction not only to divisional rugby but to Jim Syddall, the Waterloo lock who had played for England against Ireland that year. Jim had steak and tomatoes for breakfast, steak and tomatoes for lunch; he was a monster of a man and I couldn't believe how much he ate on the morning of a match. At the dinner after the game I thought the thing to do would be to sit down with Kaiava Salusalu, my opposite number, but Jim and Tony Bond, the Sale centre, demanded that I should sit opposite them, which was the biggest mistake a 19-year-old could make. Neither is exactly restrained when it comes to post-match enjoyment and I learned quickly about ducking and diving at such functions.

Before the county championship began Yorkshire played their traditional fixture with Ulster, which was my first visit to Belfast. We crossed on the ferry, the Irish Sea doing little for team morale – Martin Shuttleworth, the Wakefield full-back, had a particularly uncomfortable crossing and departed midway through the film, not to be seen again until we docked. Having arrived we made for the Forum which had then the reputation of the most-bombed hotel in Europe. Since I was not a serving officer there was no problem for the security forces other than the general one of looking after any incoming team from England, and in that respect terrorist activities in Ireland have only once provoked a problem in my experience. There was a bomb threat when Wade Dooley, John Orwin and I were all in an England team in 1985; Wade, as a policeman, and JO and I being in the RAF, were all told of the threat, allegedly from the IRA, in the president's bar at Twickenham. We were advised that if we wanted to withdraw, the Rugby Football Union would understand though it was believed to be a hoax because the 'warning' call had not come through the recognised channel.

That visit to Belfast, though, was quite an experience. We were met by the Garda and accompanied to the hotel which was ringed with barbed wire, and it was all a considerable eye-opener for a young lad.

We went to training and, looking round, I could see every now and again Army Land Rovers and sentries. It did not encourage much exploration during our free time; it was the same when England went to Bucharest to play Romania in 1989. We had been warned so much about going out by ourselves, about the probability that we would be followed wherever we went, that there was no incentive to do so. In fact we were almost frightened to do so.

Not that as a rugby player you have so much freedom to 'see' the places you visit on tour. Having had four trips to Australia has at least allowed me to get around a bit, but I don't think people realise how little spare time we have after the business of each day is done – the training, the travelling, the obligatory social occasions.

Belfast that day was another step on the ladder of experience, in that we came up against a very good Ulster side – Trevor Ringland and David Irwin in the backs, most of whom had won at least B caps, Willie Anderson, Nigel Carr and Steve Smith in the forwards. We drew 7–7 after dominating the first half and it was good preparation for the county season to come. I played opposite Trevor, who had already won four full caps, and we were to see a good deal more of each other. I had already slotted into the left-wing role, largely because no one ever suggested I should play on the other wing except on one occasion, when the under-23 team played English Students.

The opening stage of the county championship that season – a revamped competition for the fourth (or was it fifth?) time – included an enjoyable win over Lancashire (any win over Lancashire is enjoyable for a Yorkshireman) before I took temporary leave to have my nose seen to. It was only the second time I had been in hospital – when I was five I had my appendix out, but I could hardly remember that – and I went along to have the operation assuming that for the rest of my time in hospital I would be lying around in bed. Obviously with a major operation you do, but I drifted along in whatever clothes I was wearing plus pyjamas and washbag. That was fine up to the point where the duty sister came along at seven o'clock the morning after I had had the operation, whipped me out of bed and I found I had to spend the next four days during recovery wearing the same clothes around the hospital. After a while people began to avoid me. You learn from experience!

While the RAF was pondering the future of my nasal organ, the England selectors were beginning to show their hand and decided I was worth a place in the B side to play Ireland. A week before that match Yorkshire, by beating Middlesex on the Wasps' ground, reached their first county final for 19 years, though the game was a bit of a mixed bag: I scored two tries but, on the other hand, I struggled to contain Dick Cardus, the burly Wasp playing opposite me. A very direct player, he took short balls all afternoon and we were lucky that Middlesex scored only one try as a result. It was a very muddy day and we came through 18–7 with Alan Old controlling things; I looked all right from an attacking point of view, I suppose, but not so hot defensively.

It was even muddier in Belfast when we played the B international. News of my selection had come via a telephone call from John Reason of the *Sunday Telegraph* who rang up to ask me for background details of my career. I answered with a somewhat quizzical note in my voice until he said, 'Oh, didn't you know, you're playing in the B international.' It was only the second time I had spoken to that prominent rugby journalist and we have not spoken since, which perhaps illustrates why players do not have too high a regard for him. He never seems interested in hearing our side of the story but has consistently rained destructive criticism upon the players and management, regardless of what has been achieved over the last few seasons. We sometimes wonder why, if he derives as little enjoyment from the game as his writings suggest, he remains involved with it.

The B international was a brief encounter, since we met only on the Thursday, then travelled to Belfast and played. The rain fairly hammered down, which was not wonderful for either me or David Trick on the other wing. It wasn't a bad England side – Paul Rendall, Mike Teague and Dave Cusani were among the forwards while the backs included Nigel Melville and Chris Martin. I received a pass in something like the third minute but the Irish full-back read our move well and didn't have to go too far to get me, and that was the only ball I got all day – in the only B international I played.

Nigel and I both had a talking-to from Derek Morgan, one of the England selectors, about moving clubs – I was still with Middlesbrough and 'Smellie' was playing for Wakefield. He suggested we should join a club like Headingley (which tells you something about relative change in the English club structure since the introduction of leagues), that a bigger club would help for England playing purposes. Neither of us went along with the idea and for me there was hardly any point since I was joining the RAF and any move would depend on my eventual posting.

England's trial teams were announced after that 10–6 win over Ireland and I was on the bench, a left-wing watching four right-wings

– John Carleton, Tony Swift, Trickie and Barry Evans – on the pitch. At the time I was happy enough to be on the fringe; I don't think that would have happened in recent times. It turned out to be a good game to miss if you were on the junior side, since the seniors won 47–7.

Meanwhile the RAF were coming to a decision. Having heard nothing since my operation I received a telephone call out of the blue – no pun intended – asking when I wanted to start at Cranwell. I had been pencilled in for the first course in January but Yorkshire were due to play Gloucestershire at Bristol on 29 January in the county final so I asked if my joining could be deferred until after that. I didn't mind giving the rest of the season away; Yorkshire would have finished, I would have to move from Middlesbrough anyway and I wasn't going to play in the Five Nations championship. As it turned out, the big day at Bristol went Gloucestershire's way; they won 19–7, their forwards put the screws on the Yorkshire pack and their backs showed they could play a bit.

The RAF agreed and put me on 68 Initial Officer Training course starting on 14 February. There had never been the least doubt in my mind what I wanted as a career and I was pleased to find that, at last, I was able to get on with it. All I had been doing since leaving school was killing time, although I never became frustrated because I was certain in my own mind that the time would come. I tied up loose ends and played out my last games with Middlesbrough before saying goodbye to the many good friends I had made at Acklam Park (one of the great regrets of the constant rounds of representative games is that I have so seldom been able to return to watch Middlesbrough play, or catch up on the news of people I played with).

It was, though, a wrench for my mother because I was the first of the brood to leave home and it was only ten months since my father's death. It had been a devastating time for her and while she still had her hands full with the children at home, only she knows how hard it was to come to terms with her loss. That she has come through it all speaks volumes for her inner strength and I will always be grateful for her support and love. I know how much pleasure she has gained from the achievements of all four of us. It was typical of her that she took time to organise a farewell party for me on the Sunday before I left to catch the train from Darlington – on my way, if not quite airborne.

5

Per ardua ad astra

Enthusiasms are attractive features in children, even if they take up too much time and too much room in the eyes of long-suffering parents. The genuine enthusiasms of the young retain a freshness and a novelty which may be washed away by older cynicism. Rory's desire to fly was born young and remained with him; at 18 it is comparatively rare to find someone as single-minded in his ambition to join the Royal Air Force as Rory was, but it very swiftly became evident after only a few minutes' conversation.

The obvious starting point was the long flights across the world that he and Gary made when they began school in Yorkshire. The two small boys were taken up to the flight deck and, at home, Rory would write to airlines for information about aircraft and aviation. School offered membership of the Combined Cadet Force and the chance to add practical experience to enthusiasm, of which, as we have seen, Rory took full advantage.

The start to anyone's career is a major step in life but joining the services at that time was also a very serious statement of intent, since Britain had been at war during 1982. Rory had discussed with one of his England colts colleagues, Richard Taylor from Rosslyn Park, what joining the services would mean as they prepared for the game with Wales that spring. Pictures of conflict in the Falkland Islands could be seen every day on the television screens of the nation and it made no difference that the war was being fought in the South Atlantic, a long way from home, or that on the scale of such things it was not a major conflict.

Over 1000 lives were lost, a quarter of whom were British, and tensions established between Britain and Argentina which existed for the rest of the decade. Ironically, when the Rugby Football Union sent a touring party to Argentina in 1990 (a tour for which Rory was not available) they were welcomed with great warmth and expressions of regret that traditional friendships had been disrupted by the war. It seemed then, and still does, to have been an avoidable conflict but it was an additional reminder alongside the suffering of Northern Ireland that the role of the serviceman remains active in the extreme.

Joining the RAF was a bit like the first day of term at school: the list of requirements had arrived at home, including a lounge suit, which was the first time I needed one. But after the farewell party was over I set off on the train for Grantham where the newcomers are met by a service bus for Royal Air Force College Cranwell and a group of senior cadets who tick off the arrivals. It's a small world – I have spent a considerable part of my career at Grantham and both my daughters have been born there.

As a school leaver, or direct entrant, I was Officer Cadet Underwood. The student entrants joining from university were Student Officers but there is little distinction during the 18-week course which follows. I had been asked when I first went for interview at Biggin Hill what I wanted to do and, for a pilot, you can join on a permanent commission which is for 16 years or until the age of 38, so that the RAF can be sure they will get at least 16 years out of you before they give you a pension. Obviously if you are a graduate you can join when you are that much older than I was; I signed on until I was 38, which will take me up to June 2001. You can join, too, on a short-service commission which is for 12 years with an option at eight years. With hindsight I wonder if I might not have been wiser to have given myself that flexibility (since you can extend to a permanent commission if you want to) but since I did not, I have wasted no time regretting it.

We all made for No 2 mess on arrival. The previous week those who preceded us had graduated and we were the next batch of would-be officers, about 120 all told. We were split into 14 flights. Accommodation, as you might expect, was fairly basic although we all had single rooms containing bed, cupboards and sink and there I spent my first night. The first full day was basically kitting out, when you stroll around in 'civvies' collecting combat kit, camouflage gear and the like but it was, as it happened, St Valentine's Day too and we were amazed – and impressed – to find one guy had two sack-loads of mail arrive for him. Apparently the year before he had complained to a friend that no one had sent him a card and his friend had organised a relay chain urging people to send him a Valentine's Day card. It worked, too, because he had cards from all over the world.

The press found out about it so we had a couple of journalists round to see him, which all made day one quite a novelty. It took him some time to live it down! For my part I had a somewhat unexpected introduction to the Adjutant of my flight – each of the 14 has its own Flight Commander, as well as a Training Officer, Adjutant and then the Wing Commander, who's the boss. I was ordered before the Adjutant who said I had been picked to play for the RAF against Plymouth Albion on Wednesday night, that I would be picked up at 4 p.m. the next day by a Flight Lieutenant from the rugby club and driven round to Flight Lieutenant Nigel Gillingham's house at Bottesford just outside Grantham and that he would take it from there.

So the RAF rugby recruiting net had done its stuff. What do you say on your first day but 'Yes sir'? There was an element of service work the next day, completing kitting out, the odd lesson from the Flight Sergeant who taught us how to iron our kit, an essential skill for any serviceman: how to iron shirts the service way, where to put the creases in the back, using brown paper over camouflage kit so as not to raise a shine on the material, how to fold your trousers with paper over the top and put them under your bed so as to ensure permanent creases in the right places. We learned how to fold kit ready for daily inspection – everything is inspected, the hallway, the toilets, the beds, every cupboard – all part of the overall service discipline but also starting the creation of team discipline, working together as a unit. We all took part in every menial chore, cleaning loos until they were spotless, getting rid of any speck of dust on any surface which might attract it, light bulbs, pelmets – you name it, we dusted it because inspection might include an officer wearing white gloves which he would run over surfaces looking for signs of dirt. It got to the stage where some people, rather than sleeping in their bed, would use the sleeping bags with which we had all been issued because every day we had to strip the bed, both sheets and blankets, and fold everything in a neat line at the bottom of the bed so that it was all just so, squared off. The same applied to clothes in cupboards, to keeping the sink in your room shiny – everything had to comply with the service standard.

It was quite a relief when my lift arrived to take me off on the Tuesday afternoon to Nigel's house. He joined the RAF after taking a degree at Loughborough University and was a very handy lock forward who played for Leicester for several seasons. I slept at his house that night and at first light the next day we drove to Nottingham, picked up two other players and headed for the railway station to get to Plymouth. That was a real cross-country slog, to

Derby, to Birmingham and so onwards into the West Country. When we arrived I knew nobody and all they knew of me was that I was a fresh-faced England B player with a bit of a reputation. John Orwin, who later captained England, led the side, which had a bit of a run-out before the game in the evening which we lost by one point. The only other occasion I've been to Plymouth the same thing happened: the referee added extra time and we lost by a point. After the game the officers in our side were taken off to the officers' mess at HMS *Drake* and the rest of the lads went off to the barracks, and that was my introduction to an officer's life, even if it was a Naval mess. However it was important to become used to that side of the service because that, as much as anything, was what I had spent a year preparing for; I had been told after my initial test that my scores as a pilot and navigator had been good and that the technical side would present no problems at the outset, but it was that extra year of maturing that I needed to help me understand what was involved in service life.

The next day we jumped in the train and went all the way back, arriving late in the afternoon, so of my first four days in the RAF, two had been spent travelling up and down the country by train! Some people might consider that to be time wasted by the RAF, while others might suggest I was given a place because of my rugby. But I don't think that the service would put as much money as is required to train a pilot into someone they did not feel reasonably confident would both stay the course and make the grade at the end of it. The fact that I received my wings and have progressed as far as I have knocks such criticism, I hope, firmly on the head.

My first six weeks were spent in what we call 'greens', camouflage kit and corps boots. Each day we would parade outside our block, learning to make sure that no item of kit was out of place – anyone with a pocket flap showing would be shouted at by the Flight Sergeant, a fate I managed to avoid. There were times – perhaps when you were on your knees cleaning the toilets or bulling the metalwork –when you wondered what it had to do with being an officer in the air force. But it was all part of the basic discipline. My philosophy in anything is to get on and do it and much of my approach to life now was learned during that first 18 weeks in the RAF. I wouldn't accept that it's a lack of imagination, but more part of my down-to-earth attitude. I wanted to be a pilot; to be a pilot you have to be an officer, and part of officer training involves this initial opening period. And 18 weeks is not such a long time. You learn very quickly that so much of what you do is what we called BF – 'buggeration factor'. Everything the air force did was to bug you around, see how you react, learn about your mental attitude. You could compare it with being on a rugby tour: if at any stage you crack, you lose your temper, forget your sense of humour, rebel against the management or whatever, you find out in no time that you have done yourself no favours. Whenever the BF comes into play, you grit your teeth and put up with it. There was no real hardship involved but what it did was allow you to find out how the service worked.

I was finding out how the service played too. I played in a couple more warm-up games before the inter-services championship and felt I contributed reasonably well. When we came up against the Army I managed a try in our 16–7 defeat (John Orwin kicked a penalty) and we beat the Royal Navy by the less than sparkling score of 6–4. My flight at Cranwell were pretty good about my absences to play rugby; in fact throughout my service career there has hardly been any complaint when I have been away. I've heard rumours but no one has ever said anything to me directly, which I hope means that I have done my fair share of the work when I am around.

Halfway through the course we moved to No 1 mess and the discipline relaxed; we doubled up in rooms and the daily inspection became a thing of the past. Up to that stage we had been doing classroom exercises, basic leadership exercises which taught you to control the members of your group so that you worked as a team. One obvious example could be five of you doing a jigsaw puzzle in which you would detail two people to look for outside pieces of the puzzle, another to concentrate on blue for the sky and so on. We learned how to speak in public by making a short presentation, then everyone else offering criticism; in some exercises we would go into a field and build a children's playground, or erect a ten-foot-high pole, but anything we did was designed to make us work effectively as a team under the direction of whoever was nominated leader of the exercise for the day. There were navigational exercises too; at weekends we would be taken into the countryside, given a map, a compass and a grid reference and told to get from A to B, both in the day-time and during the night when we learned to use the stars as navigational aids.

At the halfway stage of officer training comes the crunch: you stay in and continue the course; you may be re-coursed because, for one reason or another, you haven't come up to scratch and have to start again; or you're out, unsuitable officer material. One person from my flight decided the night he arrived that the RAF was not for him and left the next morning, which I found very strange given the trouble he must have taken to get there in the first place; 24 hours is hardly time enough to judge that it's not for you.

Those of us continuing the course went off to what was called Camp One at Stamford PTA in Norfolk. We lived in barracks and each day was split into quarters – each six-hour period would involve a fresh exercise. Thus an instructor might say: 'Underwood, this is your lead, your mission is to establish a radio base at this location. Equipment has been left at various other locations and you have to accomplish it within this time scale.' Having received your instructions you go back and brief the other members of your flight on how best to achieve the mission. We were also introduced to the various assault course obstacles with which we would have to cope, including the pond across which we were supposed to swing on a rope before landing safely on the other side. One lad was so enthusiastic about the demonstration that he threw himself from the jetty to grab the rope swinging towards him but, unlike Tarzan, missed and belly-flopped into the water, to the huge amusement of the hundred or so of us who were standing around.

There's a lot of walking and running involved and I was fitter than I had ever been before. The first eight weeks we had done a lot of LAT (leadership and agility training) runs, either one and a half or two and a half miles, in our greens and the idea was for each flight to get round as quickly as possible. Our Flight Commander was Gordon Graham who, sadly, died in a mid-air collision in a Tornado two years ago; off we went for our run and I, of course, was supposed to be this super-fit sportsman. But long-distance running has never been my forte, particularly loaded up with webbing, and I set off at a plod while everyone else shot off into the distance. There was a lot of shouting but I just kept my head down and kept my own pace; halfway round, though, some of them were struggling and you do what these runs are designed for, help each other and make sure everyone gets home within the time allowed. That evening I received something of a dressing-down from the Flight Commander, who said how surprised he was by my fitness – or lack of it. So I suggested that while I was fairly useful at short spurts, long distances were not quite the same, and I think he took the point; people don't always appreciate that fitness can be specific to whatever activity you are engaged in. Because you can run faster than a lot of other people doesn't mean you will distinguish yourself at the marathon.

The course concluded with Camp Two, still in Stamford but now involving simulated battle conditions. One exercise brought together two sides, one of whom was carrying a 'missile', and you scored points for the length of time you retained the missile. Carrying a six-foot-long mock missile round Stamford is no fun; first you have to find the group who has it, 'dispose' of one team member to claim the missile and then make your getaway while the opposition give you a minute's grace. At the end of the week the final exercise is called 'top dog' when all 14 flights set off around a three-mile course, collecting pieces of equipment along the way – our flight panted in around the halfway mark. However, midway through the course I had to play in the inter-services game at Twickenham which, as far as my colleagues were concerned, was merely an opportunity to load me with money with which to bring back Mars bars to keep everyone going. What do they say about work, rest and play?

By that stage there were five left in my original flight and it was back to academic studies, wearing 'blues' – RAF working dress. That involves war studies, service writing – learning how to write routine paperwork with which officers are likely to be involved – running an office, day-to-day administration in which the Flight Commanders act as civilians and bring a series of problems to your door to which you are expected to provide an answer. There's a lot of marching too, all leading up to Camp Two by which time we had learned more field craft, how to control weapons, order fields of gunfire. Of our flight, four wanted to be pilots and one an engineer, but everything we had learned up to this point was to do with leadership rather than flying.

Arriving for Camp Two you are split into blue or orange forces, standard NATO war games colours, and you take part in a series of exercises all of which are exceptionally well planned and which are sometimes not what they seem. The point is to try to recreate the confusion which exists in war-time, so you might be picked up by helicopter and told you are being taken to one point, then be set down at another from which you must make your own way home. I can remember being leader in one night-time exercise when, clearly, one of the main priorities is to ensure that people are silent. I had given my briefing and we walked off into the night, carrying all our equipment with us, but I had forgotten one of the basic preparations which is to get the flight to jump up and down. That makes sure there is nothing to rattle like the knife and fork in your billycan, and that your water bottle is full so there is no chance of liquid sloshing around. So there we were, in a combat group, treading silently down a side road, whispering orders until we reached a main road we had to cross; cautious looks all round, nothing in sight, so we crossed quietly one by one until a Saudi in our group came to do so and as he ran across all we could hear was the 'glug, glug, glug' from his half-full water bottle!

However, we didn't find ourselves in a well-prepared ambush so we proceeded with our mission. Half a mile down the road we came to a stream where we had to lay some wire, but before we had finished a truck came roaring down the road so we sneaked under a bridge, only to find that they parked alongside, climbed out and started chatting away while we shivered gently by the stream. All of a sudden there was a loud 'click' as one of my group decided to cock his rifle, but he wasn't heard and eventually the lorry took off again. We could have 'attacked' them but, it being night, I didn't know whether they were blue or orange, nor did I know how many of them there were, so I decided discretion was the better part of valour.

My impression of the course was that everything seemed to be going well; both my leads had been satisfactory and I met my old Flight Commander at one stage who suggested that progress was good. After Camp Two was over we all went back for the final run-in to exams, drilling and the big day when you discover whether or not you have passed. The Flight Commanders break the news, and some of them had individual ways of doing it: one told his flight that if, when you went into his room, a little green plastic frog on his desk was looking at you, you had passed. If it was turned away, you had failed. The great eccentric English tradition lives on. Mine was more conventional: 'I have the pleasure of telling you that you passed the course.' Now we could prepare for the final parade and get our kit: parade No 1s for passing-out and No 5s, mess dress, for the function in the evening. The final parade is in front of College Hall in Cranwell, on the square beside the cricket pitch which is called the Orange: two lines of cadets come marching out from each side of the building with the aim of coming crashing to a stop at exactly the same time when the parade master calls halt. It's not easy and requires very precise timing, but happily we managed a good one. The appropriate words are spoken, there's a fly-past and then a march past the Reviewing Officer and into College Hall to the mess. Both the Flight Sergeants wait to welcome the commissioned officers as they enter: a smart salute and 'Congratulations, sir' which is the first time that anyone has called you 'sir'.

Mum came down for the occasion, with Gary, Tony and Wendy, to take part in the lunch and there's a ball in the evening. By that time you know your next posting and, after a fortnight's holiday, Acting Pilot Officer Underwood was to stay in Cranwell. Student Officers with a degree begin as Pilot Officers but for all of us there was ground school, aerodynamics, technical aspects of aircraft, meteorology, navigation, the lot, with tests thrown in all the time. That suited the graduates rather more than it did me; cramming a lot of facts into a short space of time had never been my cup of tea and assimilation of so many new elements created problems. I found myself falling behind the pre-set objectives before I went into the flying phase of 44 course in the Basic Flying Training School, flying Mark V Jet Provosts (two-seater aircraft which, at that time, were the basic instructional jets). I had done four trips when the ground school instructor decided my results weren't good enough and it was decided I should be re-coursed. So the next week I went back to square one with 45 course in the classroom; it still wasn't great but it was a lot better than the first time and I was able to fill in some of the gaps and emerged into the flying side.

Obviously I wasn't a completely natural flier but at least I was in the air again. My flying time before starting at BFTS comprised two hours in a glider, two 30-minute trips in a Chipmunk and 35 hours in a Cessna. Provosts were considerably quicker and the first time I went up I was nervous; I didn't know whether, at such a vastly increased speed, I might be scared of flying or of heights. But it's all a question of confidence and the nervous twitch didn't last long. By the time I got through the second course I had established that, if nothing more, I was a basic, average pilot.

You have 15 trips in which to establish yourself before going solo; the first ten include a lot of medium-level flying to familiarise yourself with the particular aircraft type and understand what happens if this or that control is used, if the flaps go down and so on. The next stage is coping with emergencies, how to control a stall or a spin or a flame-out (when the engine cuts out), and negotiate a forced landing, and having found your way through that you begin circuits, the process of take-off and landing and the checks through which you must go before you bring an aircraft in to land. That is a continuous programme until the instructor feels you have enough competence to go solo. The repetition suited me; my confidence increased and I was able to go solo in two trips, whereas normally you take three or four.

You quickly learn not to be too confident, though. The next step was a dual trip, with an instructor, from Cranwell to Waddington, which is about 20 miles by road but only a couple of minutes by jet. The idea is to make the short flight having done all the appropriate checks and sent out all the necessary radio calls at the correct times, but on this first occasion the aircraft was well ahead of me. I was still doing departure checks from Cranwell when I should have been preparing for landing at Waddington. It was a really bad trip and I found myself back under the microscope, which made the next two trips a bit more tense.

A new year, new ground to break. During 1983 I had received non-travelling reserve cards for England and watched on television the demise of the British Lions in the four internationals in New Zealand (a tour for which I had been asked about my availability). I had also joined Leicester which, being based at Cranwell just over 30 miles away and knowing Leicester's reputation, seemed the obvious thing to do even though Nottingham might have been slightly closer. Leicester were one of the country's top clubs, their reputation still strong after three cup wins in a row between 1979 and 1981, and they had lost the 1983 cup final to Bristol in a smashing game. The fact that the career of Tim Barnwell, their regular wing, had been ended by injury in that final had nothing to do with my decision. I wanted to join them and I had taken advice from Alan Old, who had been a playing member of Leicester in the 1970s, well before I began playing with him in Yorkshire's team; he made contact and I received a letter from Graham Willars, who was then Leicester's coach, inviting me to train at Welford Road. In fact I had already played there, for the RAF against Leicester under lights the previous season, so I had at least sampled the atmosphere.

However, joining as a playing member created an initial problem because, although I had started flying training, I didn't have a car although I had long since got my licence. That meant a visit to the bank manager to see whether I could negotiate a loan to buy a Mini Clubman that a friend was selling for £650; that seemed quite a lot of money to me at the time but I was happy to find that my reasonably thrifty habits were now paying off – literally. My deposit account was in good order which left the bank manager without too much of a decision to make, and I joined the rugby commuters.

I had met some of Leicester's players at the Selkirk sevens the previous seasons so I knew the backs like Les Cusworth, Clive Woodward and Dusty Hare, all of whom were very much in the international frame. But I served my apprenticeship, as everyone joining Leicester does, in the second XV under the guidance of Brian Hall, the centre who had captained the club to their first cup final in 1978. The first-team wings were Barry Evans, who was capped in Australia in 1988, and Kevin Williams, a Wales B player in 1981, but I was quite happy. I was playing for a senior club and although it was a totally different atmosphere from Middlesbrough the club was buoyant, even though it was the end of that long era in which they had been coached by 'Chalkie' White. His influence at Leicester had been huge but the previous year he had joined the Rugby Football Union as a divisional technical administrator, so although players still referred to what he had done, there was something of the new broom about the club.

I played the first couple of months of the season in the second team and enjoyed it. I wasn't knocking on the selectors' doors every week badgering for a place in the first XV; I accepted I was new to the club, that I was finding my feet and I had anyway no automatic expectation of a place in the senior side. But I got my chance in mid November, against Northampton at Franklins Gardens; at that time Northampton were not the power they became at the start of the 1990s but it was by no means an easy game and I noticed the step upwards in class. In particular it was a tremendous education to train and play with the Leicester back division, all of whom were internationals except Barry Evans and me. It started with Nick Youngs at scrum-half, with Les, Clive and Paul Dodge in midfield and Dusty at full-back, and in training Les pretty well ran the show. We would run through the moves, which never seemed to take too long, and the rest of the time we would think up other variations, some of which we used in matches although one, which we called the 'Hateley', we never did. That was a move in which Les lobbed up a miss-pass, Clive headed it back inwards (hence Hateley after the England footballer) and the rest of us would come steaming up to grab the ball. Another was the 'Shotgun' which saw the ball go out to Paul who put it on the floor, then Les picked up and flicked it through his legs to someone coming short from the blind side.

For me it was a fantastic education, seeing the game played with such abandon. I don't think I could have had a more unblinkered, unstereotyped experience at such a young age. The grounding at Middlesbrough had been wonderful, good positive rugby with a great bunch of players, but at Leicester you were encouraged to get on and try things and with all these experienced players around, offering positive, constructive criticism, it was superb. And you knew that if there were any problems during a game, Dusty would find touch 60 yards downfield and you could start again. It was good preparation, too, playing in the stadium at Welford Road which is the biggest in England outside Twickenham, a fantastic arena for a club side and where the members can produce an intense atmosphere.

It's difficult to convey the attitude which permitted Leicester to run the ball from five-metre scrums on their own line against a club such as Gloucester. I scored two tries at Welford Road against them; one came when we ran from within our own 22 and when I was caught, inevitably Clive was there. He broke free, Dodgie picked it up and gave it back to me and I scored under the posts. That's the best illustration of why I love playing rugby so much. Clive, for my money, was the most brilliant support runner I have had the pleasure of playing with. If I did anything and looked round he was there; he just had this knack of turning up. I never seemed to be in a position of confusion, or in a quandary about what was going on. There would be minor adjustments suggested during games – advice to stand a little wider, a little deeper – but my first two or three years at Leicester were champagne rugby, the game at its best.

The objective that first season, of course, as it is for anyone at the club, was to play in the annual game against the Barbarians at Christmas time. The previous year in the same match Barry Evans had scored three times against an out-of-sorts Mike Slemen and it had registered with me that while there were a lot of right wings knocking around England, there were not so many pushing for the left-wing position. When England played their final Five Nations match in Dublin in 1983 there had been considerable debate immediately beforehand as to which of John Carleton or David Trick should play on the left and although I had no idea how I stood in the pecking order I felt there might be a chance. Slem and JC were the men in possession, Trickie and Tony Swift were knocking around and had toured Argentina in 1981 with England and Barry couldn't have been far away.

As for me, I was comfortable with my rugby. I felt I had settled in and was perhaps even more settled after the Barbarians game which we won 30–26 with just the sort of rugby I have been talking about. Barry scored one of our four tries and I scored two more, with one disallowed after Clive had broken from behind our own posts, made ground and I managed to catch him up and run the rest of the way, only for David Burnett, the referee, to rule the pass forward. It was a tremendous spectacle and the 17,000 crowd was by far the biggest I had played in front of. Barbarians games are always the same at Leicester: you have the sense of the crowd hemming you in, the pace of the game which in the first 20 minutes leaves you gasping and thinking you will not possibly survive the next hour.

It was after that game that things started happening. Having missed the trial, in which Slem and JC played on the senior side, with Swiftie and Mark Bailey on the junior side, I was called into the training squad which met at Bisham Abbey in January. The call did not come at the most convenient moment, hard on the heels of a one-week survival exercise the RAF had thoughtfully organised in the Yorkshire Dales. Basically a group of us were thrown out and told to get on with, well, surviving. Rations were strictly limited and at the end of a week you emerge stinking to high heaven. However, release comes and as we all marched back to civilisation the first place we stopped was a pub where a pint of milk, half a steak and kidney pie and some fruit juice went down without touching the sides. I may have been ready for it but my stomach certainly was not and on the RAF bus back to base, stomach won.

However, I recovered in time to collect a lift down to the squad weekend at Bisham which was an eye-opener in many ways. I think a new sponsorship agreement had just been signed between the Rugby Football Union and Nike the sportswear manufacturers, and I was given a pair of boots and a pair of trainers. Up to that point I had always bought my own boots – Adidas as it happens – but it was all part of the new rugby-playing world to which I was about to be introduced. Part of Dick Greenwood's plans was a run round Marlow after a full Saturday training, and in my weakened condition I regret to say I was part of a group which decided to sneak off down a side street and tag on to the main group when it came back towards Bisham. So we sat around feeling vaguely guilty until it gradually dawned that no one had come by and the route must have changed, so we set off again to find Dick waiting at the gap in the hedge through which we re-entered the Abbey grounds. Clive and I received the rough end of his tongue, although at least I was able to plead lack of condition owing to my hard time in Yorkshire!

England were not involved in the first championship weekend but, having beaten New Zealand at Twickenham in November, the selectors stuck by the same team – indeed, I heard a rumour that a promise was made to that effect in the dressing room immediately after the game, even though the selection process preceding the All Blacks match had been specific to that match only. At all events, the only change was created by Paul Dodge who broke his leg and was replaced in the centre by Huw Davies; the established wing pair, Slem and JC, remained when the team to play Scotland was announced. I had never really had the opportunity to get to know Mike Slemen before, although I was aware he had had a rough deal from the

selectors the preceding year. But I was just pleased to be part of the
scene and when I watched a recording of the game – which England
lost 18–6 on an awful day at Murrayfield – I was like any other
spectator, rather than ticking off plus and minus points accumulated
by the wings.

The next weekend I played for Leicester against Newport at Rodney
Parade while the selectors mulled over injuries to Gary Pearce, Peter
Winterbottom and Huw Davies, and the form of the rest. Not that
England was to the forefront of my mind because I had been struggling
not only with my flying duties back at Cranwell but with an insistence
that I should play in station matches for Cranwell, when I was keen to
work towards games against the Cardiffs and Gloucesters. I received a
telephone call from a Wing Commander the gist of which was,
basically, that I was playing for Cranwell, which was a conflict of
interests I could happily have done without. To be frank, matters were
getting out of hand and they were beginning to affect my flying. I
didn't want to be re-coursed to get round the problem and I was
almost prepared to give rugby away so that I could gain ground with
the flying.

Eventually I was called in by the Group Captain who told me I was
to be posted to RAF Swinderby, near Lincoln, which is the airmen
recruitment initial training camp. I was to be a Flight Commander, but
it was a decision which made me very unhappy since I had visions of
going there for six weeks and then being re-coursed; it had happened
once before and I had been very distressed. Still, there was nothing for
it but to go and explain to the Squadron Leader at Swinderby that I
might be required for rugby on a large number of days. His reaction
was: 'You're a complete waste of space.' However, he found a spare
flight for me and I joined in some of the airmen's drills and spent a lot
of the remaining time on the telephone with social calls. It was to
Swinderby I returned after the match at Newport and on the Sunday I
was relaxing after dinner by watching *Our Man Flint* with James
Coburn on television when the barman came through and said there
was a phone call for me.

I took the call by the bar; it was Derek Morgan. I waited and he said,
'You know who I am?' and I admitted I knew he was chairman of
selectors. 'What are you doing tomorrow night?' he enquired – he's a
great one for the slow burner – and while I admitted I had nothing
planned I thought he wanted me as cannon fodder for the Monday
team training at Stourbridge. 'What are you doing on Saturday?' he
went on, and I asked, 'What do you mean?'

'Well,' Derek said, 'how would you like it if you were alongside Les Cusworth, Clive Woodward and Dusty Hare?' I thought, 'He means I've been picked for England,' but I asked him to repeat the question in plain English. So he said I had been picked to play against Ireland and waited for my reaction. After a while he said, 'Are you still there?' I was. I told him there were no problems and that I'd be there. No announcement was planned, though, until the next day and Derek asked me not to tell anybody. I put the phone down and walked back to the lounge with an inane grin on my face, but I was so excited I couldn't concentrate on the film. So I went back to my room saying, 'I've got to tell someone' and decided that I would call my mother, even if I could tell no one else. Immediately I got through she said excitedly, 'You've been picked for England', and I said in surprise, 'How did you know?' Derek, it turned out, had called her first to get my number at Swinderby!

6

'This may be a spoof but . . .'

English rugby failed to capitalise on the 1980 grand slam; rather than signalling the beginning of an era it proved no more than a highlight in a sea of mediocrity which existed in the 1970s and for much of the 1980s. Mike Davis, who coached the grand-slam team, referred to the relative failure after 1980 as a process which turned wine into water. Even though England came second in the Five Nations championship in 1981, they were one of three countries to win two matches and lose two while France, at Twickenham, clinched a grand slam for themselves.

Famous players – Roger Uttley, Tony Neary, Fran Cotton – concluded careers and those who were left found themselves at odds all too frequently with the Rugby Football Union's administrators and selectors. Incidents such as the 'boot-money scandal', when accusations were made that leading players in international squads received payment for wearing a certain brand of boot, were rife in 1982, a year in which England were again second in the table but behind Ireland; not that anyone begrudged the Irish their first triple crown in 33 years.

However, 1983 saw a dire decline in form, which left England propping up the championship with only one point from their four matches. That point came, ironically, from a 13–13 draw in Cardiff, England's best away result against Wales since their 1963 victory. There was considerable debate about the merits of divisional rugby and the potential of a league structure which, at that stage, was still four years away from reality. What was evident was that the game lacked direction, a situation which Richard Greenwood, Davis's successor as coach, tried to remedy by adopting a horses-for-courses policy in an effort to beat New Zealand who, at short notice after the cancellation of their scheduled tour to Argentina, were to visit Scotland and England.

England won their warm-up game against the touring Canadians and then, to intense local delight, the Midlands beat the All Blacks at Leicester. A week later England, led by the Leicester hooker Peter

Wheeler who had captained the Midlands too, beat New Zealand at Twickenham; joy was unconfined, which tended to overlook the fact that the All Blacks had left at home a complete front five plus David Loveridge, the scrum-half who had been so influential when his country in the summer of 1983 dismissed the challenge of the British Lions 4–0.

So England entered 1984, a year made difficult for a great variety of reasons. It was the year of the miners' strike, when the National Union of Mineworkers was in conflict, sometimes literally, with the Conservative Government and the police; when the nation was shocked by the shooting of a woman police officer outside the Libyan Embassy in London where terrorist gunmen were believed to be hiding. It was the year of the Los Angeles Olympic Games, boycotted by all Communist countries save Romania, and when the RFU after an agonised debate voted overwhelmingly to send an England team to South Africa, despite political advice and the vociferous calls of the anti-apartheid lobby.

England's rugby aspirations, however, were put firmly into perspective by the Scots in the first championship match of the season, which they lost 18–6. They were to win only once in the 1984 season and the touring party in South Africa, with the exception of a fine performance against Western Province, did not distinguish itself. It was the last official side to go to South Africa before the crumbling in 1991 of the legislation which kept apartheid in place. Not that history matters a jot to a young man winning his first international cap . . .

When I asked for time off because I was required for duty with England, I was properly cautious. I told my squadron boss: 'Look, this may be a spoof but if it isn't I have to be at Stourbridge training this evening and go down to London on Thursday because I've been picked to play for England.' The authorities, happily, had no objection; my job at that stage was undemanding anyway so they congratulated me and waved me on my way.

It was not so undemanding, though, that I had nothing to occupy me that Monday morning. My flight of airmen were passing out on the Wednesday and so we were going through a parade practice when the first telephone call came through. It was Terry Cooper from the Press Association who was the first to reach me after the team had been made public; not that the PA, the national news agency, meant a great deal to me when the corporal told me who was calling, but at least it told me that there was no question of Derek's call having been a spoof, or a dream in the night.

For the rest of the morning the phone didn't stop. Every time I tried to sit down for lunch a call came, one of them from Air Marshal Sir Michael Knight, the RAF's representative on the RFU committee, who was very happy to see an airman chosen. But I had had time to contact Dusty Hare, with whom I had spent a lot of time travelling to and from Leicester, and he organised my travel down to Stourbridge with the rest of the Leicester players – there were seven in the match party – involved against Ireland. That alone made sure that I didn't feel as though I was in a totally new environment. I had met most of the other players and the other new cap, Bryan Barley from Wakefield, had played with me in the Yorkshire back division. It may say something about my eating habits, or service cooking, that the best part of that first evening was the meals they laid on at Stourbridge after training, which were excellent.

Kitting out then was not so involved, or generous, as it is now. Today's players receive blazers, slacks and casual gear as well as some of the basic rugby kit whereas that week I trained initially in my old colts kit before the meeting on Thursday. Tuesday and Wednesday turned into an extended photo call because a pilot in the national team was something of a novelty – Peter Glover from Bath had played on the wing 13 years earlier; Peter Larter, the Northampton lock, made the last of his England appearances in 1973 and Billy Steele (Bedford) had played on Scotland's wing in 1977 but the services were drying up as a source of supply. It was a bit embarrassing but I can't recall any major hurdles, apart from requests to pose alongside the jet I normally flew: since I wasn't flying, because of the rugby, that was a problem but an aircraft had to appear somewhere. One of the photographers had me scrambling over a Chipmunk, the most basic of propeller-driven trainers which flies around at 100 mph, but they had to make do with that because though there was some talk of having a Jet Provost flown up, the weather wasn't wonderful either and that fell through. At the same time the flight was supposed to have its dress rehearsal for passing out, their big day, and there had to be time given over to that.

Considering my lowly status in the RAF at the time the headlines were a little hard to swallow: 'Jet Ace' was the typical description – would that it had been true – but the best of all was in *The Sun* which had the jet ace with his Chipmunk, which must have caused a few ripples over breakfast in RAF messes up and down the country. Their story had the flying ace, based at 'RAF Swindelbury' in Leicestershire (not Lincolnshire), receiving his wings in a passing-out parade the next day – everything about it was wrong. I went back to Cranwell that evening to meet old friends from my flying course for a drink and we had a good laugh about all the publicity.

The second half of the week, however, was sterner stuff. But the preparation was made so much easier with Dusty keeping an eye on me all the way – we even roomed together at the Petersham Hotel in Richmond. Les called the shots in training – after the criticism directed at the team which lost in Scotland his attitude was to shrug it all off and emphasise the importance of playing the way we wanted to. Clive Woodward and Nick Youngs were there too, with Peter Wheeler as captain and Steve Redfern, who turned to rugby league later that season, the replacement prop, all from the same club. Dusty's first action was to throw his bed out of the room so that he could sleep on the mattress on the floor to ease his bad back, but it was so relaxing to have his familiar presence, no heavy advice but just the odd word to keep me aware of what was required.

It was the only season in which England tried to exploit the Leicester backs *en masse* and it didn't really come off. Once you take away the timing and understanding which club sides can achieve, you reduce the effectiveness of the players. At Leicester the backs played the way they did because they had to survive on limited possession and it became an automatic response. England, with a solid set piece, had alternatives to offer but had yet to make effective use of the second, third and fourth phase ball.

When we do sessions nowadays we work out the consequences, rather than organising a crash through the middle hoping to make the right response. When I began the backs practised their moves, the forwards practised their moves and we came together at the end. I suppose you could say we came together at the end against Ireland; it was quite an expansive game but we didn't score any tries. What Derek Morgan described as 'one of the most exciting back divisions in English rugby over the last couple of years' emerged with a 12–9 win, three penalties and a dropped goal against three penalties.

My major worry beforehand was whether I would become very nervous, but that didn't happen and seldom does on the day of the game. I had the odd attack of butterflies in the stomach travelling down in the car and when we gathered as a team in Peter Wheeler's room to focus on the game, all of us together in one room with no outsiders, and everything coming home to you. But once we got on the bus to go to Twickenham there were no problems. I enjoyed the new experience of outriders clearing the way, although they're not a patch on the French ones, and the arrival at the West Car Park crammed with people. I enjoyed the spectacle rather than thinking of the implications of why they were all there. I think it was the first time I had used the home changing room because the RAF, the junior service, was always given the away room at inter-service matches; there were the England jerseys, hanging on each peg, but the biggest moment was going out on to the pitch beforehand to the roar from the crowd.

To an extent I had experienced big crowds before, at Leicester, but this was four times the size and the hairs rose on the back of my neck. It's always the same at Twickenham: when the first white shirt appears in the tunnel the cheers start and as you run out it rises to a crescendo and it's a good feeling, it always is. You wait for the anthem and then there you are – starting your first international match. It was quick, partly because internationals always are and partly because Les wanted to run everything. I went into it with a niggling ankle injury and after 20 minutes I tripped over John Hall and had to receive attention, but all I could think of was that, whatever happened, I wasn't going off in my first international.

The game ended with me perched on Trevor Ringland's shoulders. He was my opposite number and the final act of the match was the two of us chasing after a loose ball into the dead-ball area under the North Stand. He got there first, I went down on him and he got up immediately and, because he's quite a chunky lad, I went up with him. Then the whistle went and we shook hands – when he let me down – and turned to go off when there was a whack across my shoulder-blades. Some of the crowd had run on the pitch and one of them had just given me a massive pat on the back; they weren't carrying us off in those days! Obviously the spectators were pleased but my initial reaction was disappointment with my own performance, that I hadn't been able to score. I've always been reasonably self-critical and there is always time after a game, driving back in the car or on the bus, to go through what you might have done – or might not have done. But I don't dwell on it because there's no point. What's done is done. Sometimes you can talk it through, as I had tended to do with Dusty driving back and forth to Leicester for games.

The rest of the team were pleased enough to have won, after the defeat in Scotland, and I had the satisfaction of having played for England, of receiving my player's tie in the changing room, and then receiving my cap at the reception at the Hilton Hotel in central London. At that stage you don't know much about the formalities; I just climbed into my dinner jacket and, at the appropriate moment, went up to get my cap from the president, who was Ron Jacobs that year. Ron had been with the under-23 party in Italy so I knew him – though I didn't imagine the cap itself would be so small. Still, I wore it up to the time we sat down for dinner but I knew it was something to treasure and, as soon as I could slip away, I rushed up to my room so that it would be safe.

In those days each 'alickadoo' has his own guests at a dinner table, with four players, two from each team – in our case the four wings from the game – and Trevor spent the evening trying to force Guinness down my throat. He does it every time we meet; he knows I don't drink so he tells me he didn't drink until he discovered Guinness. Not drinking, which is not so unusual for a rugby player as it used to be, is merely a matter of personal preference. Once when Yorkshire were returning from Belfast and we had compulsory left-handed drinking, Ian Hill, the Wakefield flanker, caught me out (I had caught him out earlier in the evening) and although I was on orange juice, he insisted I had to drink Guinness as my 'punishment'. I managed to get the sentence down to a half-pint but even that was bad enough. If it doesn't sound too obvious, I just don't like the taste. Beer, wine, it's all the same.

I didn't have a partner but I was still savouring the moment. Part of the realisation that you are an international sportsman occurs only when you go back to your normal existence and all sorts of different people want to talk about it; in those days too I would eagerly lay my hands on the newspapers to see what sort of a mention I got. I had kept scrapbooks earlier but that again is something that I gave up doing the more I played.

The main concern was that I should be picked again. There was no thought of a long run, merely the avoidance of the dreaded 'one-cap wonder' tag, and being in a winning side was bound to help. Our next game was against France, in Paris, and in fact the only change was the restoration of Peter Winterbottom at flanker, in place of David Cooke, the Harlequin. The fortnight passed quickly before my first visit to the French capital, though it was not so happy a visit as those the England teams of 1980 and 1982 had made. But my immediate impression was one of style, as the coach swept past the Palace of Versailles and up to the Trianon Hotel where England usually stay, some 15 miles from the centre. That means, too, a memorable journey to the Parc des Princes on match day; no one who has experienced that talks about anything but the French police outriders. Les and Clive had advised me to sit near the front of the team coach so that I could watch, open-mouthed, as they forced any traffic coming in the opposite direction out of the way. They certainly have style.

I still find the atmosphere at the Parc quite distinct from any other ground I have played at. Because the stands completely circle the ground there is an intense hissing, whistling noise; when I had watched matches there on television I had thought it was something to do with the reception but when you're there live you realise it's an amalgam of many things, of the crowd whistling, instruments playing, fire crackers – I don't find it a hostile ground. Some people might find it intimidating but I was just astonished by the spectacle and the noise, and to find that it was exactly as it sounds on television.

My opposite number that day was Jacques Bégu, from Dax, who was winning his first cap. He scored one of five French tries in a 32–18 win but I prefer to remember it for my own first international try. We were well in the match until the second half, when France scored 13 points very quickly, and they did so immediately after Dusty had converted my try which gave us, very briefly, the lead. There was a loose maul and suddenly the ball appeared from the side. Peter Wheeler did a neat job of shepherding Jerome Gallion, their scrum-half, out of the way and I took it on with my foot – those days playing football with Dad in Ipoh paid off. Then there was some space so I picked it up and started running; I fended off Bégu and went straight for the corner with the cover coming across like a train. However I could feel the last defender, Serge Blanco, might catch me so I stopped and cut back inside him before running round to the posts. You can imagine my feelings as I trotted back after putting the ball down. In retrospect it seemed to bring the best out of the French and they cantered away with the match, although we did score a late try through Dusty, which took him to 200 points in internationals.

Even though we lost I was much happier with my game than I was against Ireland. My defence went particularly well and several times when I had three or four Frenchmen running at me I was able to close them down by drifting across; once I was able to pile Bégu into the corner flag although his cross kick, a tactic which the French have always used very successfully, produced a try for Didier Codorniou. France, though, provided the benchmark in those days and the fact that we had held them for an hour made a lot of people happy in the England camp (they went on to play Scotland for the grand slam – and lost). It didn't stop the selectors making a couple of changes for the final match against Wales, though: Andy Dun, captain of the under-23s in Italy two years earlier, came in for his only cap on the flank and

ABOVE LEFT: *At home with Mum and Dad, Ipoh, Malaya, 1963*

ABOVE RIGHT: *One of the rare moments when the family was together in the same place at the same time, 1976*

BELOW LEFT: *Trying hard to look intellectual, Ipoh, 1967*

BELOW RIGHT: *Blackpool, 1990. The Underwood family – me, Wendy, Mum, my sister Wendy, Gary and Tony*

OPPOSITE PAGE: *Both Rob Andrew and I played in the rugby and cricket teams every year at school, and Rob was invariably captain*

ABOVE: *A great moment for the Underwood family. One of two games in which Tony and I played international rugby at Twickenham together. Baa-baas v All Blacks, 1989*

ABOVE RIGHT: *Huw Davies and I having a dance during the 1987 County Championship Final*

RIGHT: *The first of my 35 tries for England, Parc des Princes 1984*

LEFT: *Air Marshall Sir Micha Knight presenting me with m wings, RAF Valley, 1985*

MIDDLE: *Friends form the Guard of Honour outside St. Peter's Church, East Halton, 19 September 1987*

BELOW: *The BA simulator at Heathrow – trying to show Will and Jerry what flying a plane is all about. They both managed to land the jumbo simulator even though Jerry broke an engine off when he landed*

RIGHT: *Canberra T.17, a handsome looking beast affectionately known by 360 Squadron as the 'Warthog'*

FAR RIGHT: *Now I'm flying tl Hawk with 100 Squadron at RAF Wyton before moving o through the fast jet system, again!*

BELOW RIGHT: *Echo Mike is the oldest flying Canberra at 41 years old. Here I am flyin; EM with a couple of F-3s fro 29 Squadron*

LEFT: *Trying to hand off Australia's Ian Williams during one of our many tussles*

BELOW: *The England boys who helped the Lions win the Test series in Australia, 1989: (back) Jerry Guscott, Rob Andrew, Dean Richards, Wade Dooley, Paul Ackford, Mike Teague; (front) Brian Moore, Leo the Lion and me*

RIGHT: *Dean, Rob, Ieuan Evans and Brian join me celebrating after beating Australia at Sydney to win the series 1–2*

OPPOSITE BELOW LEFT: *Relaxing in Nadi Fiji with Will and Jeff Probyn before the England game against Fiji B, which we lost*

OPPOSITE BELOW RIGHT: *Apart from rooming together, Jerry and I used to play a lot of golf*

'The best support player I have known' – Clive Woodward takes up his support
position

Les Cusworth presenting me with the Daily Mirror 'Sports Moment of the Week'
award at the Tigers

Paul Rendall made his debut at loose-head prop. It was not a wonderful match, Wales winning 24–15 and Adrian Hadley scoring the only try after Bleddyn Bowen had stepped inside Les.

No one could claim it had been a good season – won one, lost three – but I was just pleased to have been there. 'Even if I get binned now,' I thought, 'I've still got three caps.' Many players have gone through long careers without getting even that many. People seemed to think I had been a useful addition, largely on the strength of that one try in Paris. So I was happy for myself.

I had limited horizons at that stage. However the next stepping-stone, in theory, was the proposed tour to South Africa which was a major hurdle. Less than a fortnight after the championship was over, the RFU committee met to decide whether to accept an invitation to go, in a climate which was still clouded by debate over the extent of change in South Africa. The Springboks had not visited Britain since 1970 and although Lions tours had been maintained, and Ireland had gone there in 1981, the feeling was growing that a tour might create more trouble than it was worth. As it happened the RFU decided to go, by 44 votes to 6, which among other consequences brought trouble for Leicester where the Labour-controlled council was urged to withdraw the use of the club's Welford Road ground in support of their policy of severing sporting links with South Africa.

I had already spoken to Sir Michael Knight about the tour, from a service point of view. The problem lay with the fact that the Government was my employer and they upheld the Gleneagles Agreement of 1977 which 'advised' against contact. John Orwin, the lock who was then a corporal in the RAF, had gone with Gloucester to South Africa but he had been told that he went as a private individual, not as Corporal Orwin. I knew the situation and, at the same time, I knew there had to be some concentrated work on my flying career and so I resolved that, when the international championship and the inter-services championship were over, I would get back to work in a big way. As it happened the weather during February and March had been bad, with limited flying opportunities for other members of my course and therefore less for me to catch up on.

Even so I was slightly behind in terms of flying time and the course was due to finish in September so if I took four weeks off, I would definitely have to be re-coursed. I would love to have toured with England but there were other things which were more important to me. At the same time an article had appeared in the *Daily Mail* which roundly declared that I would not be available to tour; that helped to take the decision out of my hands because once a delicate situation attracted too much publicity, the almost inevitable result was that I had to step back from it. Whether, if I had been insistent, the Government would have turned down an application to go I will never know.

My own view, as a Eurasian, of the situation as it was then was formed partly from having lived my first eight years in an Asian community where I spoke English and was regarded as a European, as a white. At school in Barnard Castle I recall being asked directly during a divinity lesson what I knew of apartheid; I didn't know and nor, it seemed, did the rest of the class, or if they did they didn't respond. That was around the age of 14, and the teacher explained what prohibitions acted against the coloured population in South Africa.

There is no justification for discriminating against people on the grounds of colour. The problem rugby had was to decide whether, by staging a tour, the game was supporting apartheid. The popular excuse was that, by going, you were able to see for yourself what conditions were like – insofar as that is realistic in the context of a tour. Whether the boycott on sporting and cultural links created the conditions for the changes which have taken place over the last three years, whether it was the release from prison of Nelson Mandela, the African National Congress leader, or the change in the leadership of the ruling National Party, or a combination of all those things, I don't know and I'm not qualified to make the judgement. What did seem strange was that another country with a bad human rights record, the USSR, was playing football against England at Wembley at much the same time as England were supposed to be playing South Africa at rugby. As far as 1984 was concerned, in practical terms it would have been ill advised of me to tour and the opportunity to go to South Africa since then has not arisen; the 1989 Lions were asked as a body how many of them might take part in the invitation party which helped the South African Rugby Board celebrate its centenary, but I could not make myself available for that.

I still feel that I should have the freedom of choice to decide and it remains a source of regret that I have never had the chance to play against the Springboks. The nearest I have come was, as it happens, the game in September 1984 against a President's XV which celebrated 75 years of rugby at Twickenham, when five South Africans, including the two coloured players Errol Tobias and Avril Williams, played. Two years later, when the International Rugby Football Board celebrated its centenary, I played for a British Lions XV at Cardiff against the Rest of the World who included Schalk Burger at lock, and three days later for the Five Nations XV at Twickenham against the Overseas Unions who fielded Danie Gerber, Carel du Plessis, Naas Botha and Flippie van der Merwe. Both times I was on the losing side!

As it was I withdrew from the argument and was on the sidelines as Peter Wheeler made himself unavailable for business reasons to lead England to South Africa – a decision which effectively ended his international career – thus joining other experienced players like Maurice Colclough, Colin Smart and Clive Woodward who could not find the time. My rugby ended after the inter-services championship, which produced a three-way tie, and I returned to flying.

I was able to establish the sort of continuity I had not had before, which helps any activity. It did not suddenly turn me into a star performer but I was able to become 'Mr Average' of the air. My particular problem was instrument flying, which requires concentration on the dials in the cockpit, assimilating information as quickly as possible and reacting accordingly; it all depends on how much your brain can absorb and still produce an automatic response, and experience of flying helps the process. At that stage my capacity was not sufficiently developed, although I never failed one of the flying tests during the course.

That process starts as soon as you go solo, with what we call 'spin-aeros', demanding basic general competence in the handling of the aeroplane. At that stage the 'baby budgies' really get airborne, climbing through cloud to find some height, as opposed to clogging up the circuit at lower level. Assuming you are successful you are awarded a CPC – a Cloud Penetration Certificate – which qualifies you to climb through 3000 feet of cloud in a straight line. Then you go into basic instrument flying and the basic handling tests, and the latter were very encouraging. Indeed, one of my former instructors, who came back to take some of the handling tests, told me: 'You know, when you first started I didn't think you were going to make it. But I was very impressed with your trip today.' After all the trials and tribulations it was good to hear that kind of comment, and to get the score he gave me.

You do about 100 hours on the basic flying course and at that stage, if you haven't been kicked out (and one person on my course asked to leave, for personal reasons), you move into different streams: for those who want to fly fast jets, for the multi-engined aircraft or for helicopters. The specialists in those three disciplines arrived to discuss the best options and it proved a very nerve-wracking time, because I wanted to fly fast jets – all my ambitions had been centred upon that. We were all called in and told that two of us were destined for helicopters, group three flying, while the rest of us went for group one – the jets. That was a huge relief because it meant I stayed in the direction I wanted to go. The relevant statistics suggest that if 200 people apply, only one may end as a single-seat, fast-jet pilot. I have since found out that I was one of a group considered far from certain to come through but worth taking the risk with.

The group one trainees face fifty hours' flying, more low-level navigation at 300 knots, formation flying, general handling. I'm a good applied flier and once we arrived at the applied flying phase, it was very enjoyable. Much of the work you might describe as flying by numbers. Thus in a steep turn you fly at 60 degrees angle of bank, through 360 degrees at the same height of 15,000 feet, holding the angle all the way, which on paper might seem easy but you are working in three dimensions. When I first started, at half that angle of bank, I found myself moving up and down through two or three hundred feet; if you think about it, that's quite a height. Obviously it doesn't happen nearer the ground where you have something to fix on, but your accuracy grows with experience.

Towards the end came the final navigation test, which may take the form of flying as though to bomb a specified target, land at another airfield, then fly back. I scraped through, and went on to the final handling test, the climax of the whole course. Again my mark was good and, despite having been so many flying trips behind the rest, I was the first to finish the course. Looking back I don't think the time spent on rugby had too great an effect because not much flying had taken place in my absence; what it might have done is concentrated my mind on doing well during a period when I was able to achieve greater continuity than before. Everyone knew I was behind and kept pushing me – 'Underwood, yes, two trips a day' – so I was flying all the time and it worked in my favour.

The course ended in September and the next course was not until March 1985, at Valley in Anglesey. The backlog was just the result of the system and we were all given holding posts; in my case it was Scampton, near Lincoln, where they flew Jet Provosts and I would still be able to play rugby at Leicester. I was given the news a couple of days after England had played the President's XV to celebrate 75 years of Twickenham – a match in which Rob Andrew was among the replacements. I returned with him and stopped overnight at his digs in

Cambridge before going on to hear that the RAF wanted to rush me through to the earliest possible course, then on to the Chivenor course which ended in December, before the next Five Nations championship.

Scampton is the instructor factory for the RAF and you go on hold, doing mundane office jobs with the odd trip thrown in. The instructors, after all, have to practise on someone but it gave me the chance of a refresher course on Provosts before going to Valley. It was also handy to have Dusty only 20 minutes away to share the travelling to and from Leicester. I'd drive down to his farm where Lesley, his wife, would have a cup of tea and a slice of chocolate cake waiting, and off we'd go. You get to know people pretty well in those circumstances and it recalled the times I'd spent travelling to train with Yorkshire, much of the time in the company of Alan Old, who was very outspoken and always generated a healthy debate about the game. They were so valuable to me in that they gave me a sounding board, an older person with whom to share problems; I respected their views, whether I agreed with them or not. It gave me a tremendous insight into rugby and the people who make up the game.

Those few months were a wonderful, unpressured time. The work at Scampton was not demanding, I shared the duties with another guy in the same situation, working out our own shift pattern, and the rugby was fun. I played a lot of RAF rugby too, almost every game going, and that year we won the inter-services championship. I was single, no ties and life had endless possibilities. Every team I played with seemed to want to move the ball, as did one notable team I played against – the 1984 Australians, who left such a vivid impression as they knocked off all four countries on the last grand-slam tour.

I could still remember the buzz there had been at school during the visit of the previous Australian touring party of 1981–82, which had included the three Ella brothers, Mark, Gary and Glen. Now Mark Ella was back again and with him the young wing who had made such an impression during Bledisloe Cup matches against New Zealand, David Campese. When I saw the itinerary I realised there was a prospect of playing against them four times – for the Combined Services and the North; I hoped to retain my England place and, having played for the Barbarians for the first time on their Easter tour at the end of the previous season, there was the possibility of playing in the end-of-tour finale at Cardiff. The Combined Services match was an early warning of what to expect, since they scored 44 points against us and most of the afternoon was spent covering across and tackling anything in a golden jersey that moved.

They obviously enjoyed their day at Aldershot; apart from anything else the playing surface at the Military Stadium there is good and the after-match function held at the Officers' Club is unlike anything else touring sides generally encounter. The band comes in and both teams have a good chance to mingle because there is not a vast amount of space and by the time the playing parties, match officials and so on have been accommodated there's not much room left. It turned into a really good evening, and Australians are pretty easy-going; the first of several friendships could be said to have started there. For example, I have a lot of time for Michael Lynagh whom I find a very straight-down-the-line person, and later in the tour I enjoyed the company of Ross Reynolds, the Manly No 8 who missed out on the internationals.

Australians enjoy playing the expansive game, although they can be as tactical in their approach as any team. But on that tour they had a big, mobile pack and one of the best orchestrators of a game in the world in Mark Ella; not only that, but his backing-up was superb. In retrospect England were lucky to meet them early in the tour; had that international come later on, with the team England fielded, we would have lost by far more than the 19–3 margin by which we were beaten. England, after the South African tour during which both inter-nationals were lost – by distinct margins – were undergoing a change in personnel. Dusty had retired from international rugby, John Scott did too, and the team put together to play Australia wore a very newly scrubbed look, although it was notable for the introduction to international rugby of Nigel Melville, the Yorkshire scrum-half who was made captain in his first game.

It's worth remembering, too, that we see the Australians once every few years and they form a dramatic contrast with Five Nations rugby which tends to be more limited in ambition. If you put together good players and a very competent coach in the circumstances of a long tour – and theirs was the last such tour – and they develop in confidence and in the style of rugby they play, they are likely to be a very attractive bunch by the end of the tour. Scotland, who had just won the grand slam, played them last and conceded 37 points. I met Alan Jones, their coach, several times and found him easy to get on with; I enjoyed hearing what he had to say – and he didn't hold back in that respect.

Perhaps it was as well that I was lucky enough to play four times against them because it wasn't until the Barbarians match that I managed to get across their line. That was an achievement rare in the English section of their tour; they played six matches in the country and only Mickey Harrison, with a run nearly the length of the

Waterloo pitch for the North, scored a try against them. The Australians beat the Baa-baas 37–30, six tries against five, and I was very happy to get one of them; the video shows my pleasure because I thumped the ground in delight. The crowd did get restless, though, because there was quite a lot of obstruction which the referee, René Hourquet, failed to penalise but I remember it for the many times the Australians were able to cut through and pour players into support.

If you ask whether that tour had a marked effect on the way we played the game in Britain, I would have to say no because all the teams I was playing for at the time – Leicester, Yorkshire, the North, the RAF – had the same positive approach. The higher up the ladder you go the harder it is to play with that kind of fluid movement, because of the better opposition you meet and, perhaps, the consequences of failure.

It was all in stark contrast to the next touring team to arrive in the country – the Romanians, of whom we knew little. In pre-World Cup days certain assumptions tended to be made about the non-International Board countries, even though in this case Romania had achieved good results in the recent past against Wales and France. They opened against the North on a dreadfully wet day at Birkenhead Park and we won quite comfortably. An awkward decision awaited the selectors because they had picked John Carleton against the Australians, but Simon Smith was pressing his claims to the right wing, as was Mickey Harrison; Rob Andrew, in his final year at Cambridge, was also knocking heavily at the door. Rob played his first game for Yorkshire that season, against Lancashire at Headingley, and we thrashed them; we had kept in touch since school and every so often we would meet back at Barnard Castle. We played together for the North against both the Australians and the Romanians before the new year brought an almost entirely new team.

The XV to play Romania was announced on New Year's Day after they had played the South and South-West at Gloucester; I drove down to that match with Mike Weston, the former centre who was chairman of the England selectors, and that was the day that Wade 'Who?' was announced to the rugby public at large. Wade Dooley has since made sure that most people in rugby know exactly who he is. I can honestly say I could not remember him from the North game at Birkenhead Park, when he came on as a second-half replacement, but there he was, the bearded 6 ft 8 in Blackpool policeman – quite a noticeable figure, you would have thought – of whom few people outside Preston had heard. Paul Dodge was named captain and there were first caps for Rob, Simon Smith, Kevin Simms and Richard Harding, as well as Wade. There were only six survivors from the team that started against Australia, which is an indication of the extent of change during the mid 1980s, and that was subsequently reduced to four by injury and illness. As a result John Orwin was capped for the first time, giving the RAF two representatives.

I was delighted that Rob had made it into the team. He displaced Stuart Barnes, whom I had known from the previous three years, which was hard on Stuart but I was bound to be biased in favour of one of my oldest friends with whom I had played at school and beyond. Rob had enjoyed a particularly good university match for Cambridge and had come into the divisional side with some success; now he was part of a young set of backs with Dodgie and Richard Harding, both very experienced, calling the shots. We ran the ball at Romania from the off, really uninhibited play which earned an early dropped goal for Rob, but the game came to reflect a certain lack of direction which I believe was characteristic of English rugby at the time.

It was an odd season, too. Bad weather meant that England played two successive home matches before going to Dublin and Cardiff. We should have started in Dublin but snow caused the game to be postponed 24 hours before kick-off; it was a bit unreal to be at the team hotel at breakfast-time and to be told of the postponement, because it happens so rarely. Most of the boys retreated to the bar before thoughts turned to the match with France in which, even though it was at Twickenham, our visitors were expected to run up a cricket score. In fact we played a 9–9 draw, two penalties and a dropped goal by Rob to go with his 18 points against Romania. Maybe we were relaxed by Bob Hesford, from Bristol, who was playing No 8; Bob fancied himself as a comedian and, aware that few people knew anything about Wade Dooley, as we drove into the West Car Park Bob mouthed out of the coach window at the milling crowds, 'W-a-d-e D-o-o-l-e-y, W-a-d-e D-o-o-l-e-y,' pointing at this big, bearded figure as he did so. We all fell about and poor Wade had to suffer that for the rest of the season. We also derived a certain amount of motivation from Ian Robertson who, in his Radio Two preview, wrote off England completely. Robbo came round to the changing room afterwards, possibly to get an interview and certainly to apologise, but it was a mistake on his part; he ended in the bath.

That is the game which most people remember for Richard Harding's tackle on Patrick Estève, which knocked the ball from his hands while he was running round behind our posts to touch down a try; we might have had a try too but Simon Smith couldn't quite stretch into the corner in one of those situations where, as a wing, you have to forget the cover, forget everything and go for it. I've acquired a reputation for getting over in tight situations whereas Smithie's style was to go in a crouch, which leaves you open to the tackle into touch. All very well to criticise others but I might have unwittingly given France the game by failing to find touch with a couple of minutes left; at 9–9 Jean-Patrick Lescarboura, the French stand-off half, had already dropped three goals and was gauging the posts for another when Philippe Dintrans, his hooker, knocked on and the chance went. I didn't appreciate it at the time but Mike Weston made very sure afterwards that I was aware of the possible consequences.

Nowadays we would have considered such a result disappointing, but at that time we were delighted even though we were the home side. We were even more pleased to emerge from the Scottish game with a 10–7 win, even though the game itself was far from outstanding. Wales should have been next on the agenda but that game too was frozen off, so suddenly we found ourselves with three championship points out of four and the Calcutta Cup in our grasp. It all came unstuck when we returned to Ireland, who were themselves playing for the triple crown in what was (at last) my first match at Lansdowne Road. There was a certain novelty value, too, though the purpose behind it was serious enough, in having a 'minder' for each of the police or service men in the team: Wade, John Orwin and me. Whether or not the IRA threat against us was a hoax, no risks were taken and a police presence at the team hotel is more or less taken for granted now. At the time it was not as disconcerting as it might seem, partly because being in the RAF accustoms you to the idea of security and people carrying out their orders and partly because as a player you are concentrating so much on the game that you tend not to notice the additional care for your welfare. Looking on the lighter side, it can be positively beneficial because the police job is to look after the visiting team wherever they go, so a lift is easily negotiated and the break in routine for the policemen involved is welcome.

My abiding impression of the game is the first five minutes when the ground seemed to be swarming with green shirts, coming at you from all angles. The result emphasised how small the gap is between championship winners and also-rans; Ireland won 13–10 but scored the winning dropped goal with only a couple of minutes to go. Earlier I had scored my second international try, a pretty close-run thing when Dodgie put in a long diagonal and the ball bounced favourably for me as I was challenged by Brian Spillane, the Irish No 8. It was a move going left from a scrum fairly deep but what helped was that Hugo MacNeill, their full-back, thought we were going to try a blind-side move and went across to cover before Paul used the big open side.

At all events our own brief glimpse of a triple crown had been blown away by the time we arrived at Cardiff for the match with Wales, played in the third week of April which, though by no means unique, is unusually late. Too late for us, as a game in which we led for much of the first hour slipped away as a result of our own mistakes – and I can speak with feeling in that respect, having made one or two myself at the Arms Park. On this occasion it was Chris Martin, the Bath full-back, in his only season of international rugby, who allowed a high ball from Jonathan Davies to bounce and then dropped the rebound on our line leaving Davies to score. Chris was big, strong and very hard to tackle but he had already had an awkward experience in Ireland when Brendan Mullin had charged down a clearance to score. The Welsh may have felt he was worth picking on again and that try took them ahead for the first time in the game, which they won 24–15.

That was my first experience of Wales's international ground and the particular mystique attached to England's games against them. I have to say it is not an occasion I enjoy; the playing surface has never been firm in all the matches I have played there, and that is particularly true for a wing because the stand roof on the players' entrance side casts a shadow which affects the consistency of the ground. Dublin is the same; the pitches I enjoy are Murrayfield and Parc des Princes, although Twickenham is good now that the grass is mown shorter than used to be the case. There was no question of being overawed on my first visit but the build-up was such, combined with England's dismal record there, that it came as almost a surprise to find that the game itself was much the same as any other.

It was a disappointing conclusion to the rugby, though flying duties offered an immediate escape. I had already started my course at Valley and enjoyed the possibly unique experience of being flown to the Welsh match by jet – there is not much room in a Hawk for rugby gear – and returning the same way from RAF St Athan, just outside Cardiff. That was only my third trip in a Hawk. I pondered whether or not to send the travel bill to the Rugby Football Union (it costs roughly £2000 to put a Hawk in the air for an hour) just to see what sort of reply I received from Air Commodore Bob Weighill, who was the RFU secretary, but I never got round to it!

Those same duties put England's tour to New Zealand that summer out of court. I had already received advice from Dusty Hare and Clive Woodward about the benefits or otherwise of touring New Zealand, since they had been there with the Lions in 1983; broadly speaking they suggested I would not be missing anything. That may be a bit dismissive of the people and the country but it is not the liveliest place to go and, if you hit a bad winter, it can be downright trying. I still have no regrets at never having toured there; I am happy to have played against them, for the Barbarians and for England in the World Cup, but I have never felt the need for a closer acquaintance.

It did leave an opening to visit Italy with the Baa-baas, though. I had toured in Wales with them the previous Easter and, as a youngster of 20, I was delighted to receive an invitation to play for such a famous club. But at that stage their place in the rugby world was changing and they were finding greater difficulty in attracting players for the traditional holiday tour; in addition I came to have reservations about whether their games were organised for the benefit of the players or for those who run the club. Perhaps today's players have slightly less feeling and affection for the traditions which the club's administrators cherish, but I did not find it the most relaxing experience.

I enjoyed the games, particularly that against Swansea in which I played outside Jamie Salmon and Kevin Hopkins, who went on to become Swansea's captain. It was the first time I had met Jamie (who did go to New Zealand, for whom he won his first international caps before he returned to England) and the two of them gave me so much space and good ball that it was an absolute pleasure. But the impression I had at the end of the weekend was not so good; it was made perfectly clear, for instance, that you were expected to take part in the golf competition on the Sunday, which scuppered plans I had for driving to Oxford and I was really upset. Not at having to play golf, when I ran up against Des Fitzgerald and Harry Harbison, the Irish front-row forwards, for the first time and had great fun, but at having a timetable laid out for me, including attendance at dinner at a prescribed time.

I did as I was told but it left a sour taste. If I felt so strongly about it, you might say, why turn out for them in the future, as I did against the Australians later in the year and then in Rome when they played Italy? A case of double standards, perhaps, but as players most of us are selfish to a greater or lesser extent and want to appear in the big matches – and the end-of-tour game awarded to the Barbarians is one of those. Appearances since then have been limited to the game against the 1988 Australians and against New Zealand the following year when the original Barbarian selections on the wing were David

Campese and Tony, my brother. It was only when Campo pulled out that the Baa-baas asked me to play and I was in two minds about it because it clashed with a league weekend – Rob Andrew had already said he was not available because he believed he should captain Wasps in their league fixture – only for Geoff Windsor-Lewis, the Barbarians' secretary, to announce that he had already spoken to John Allen, Leicester's secretary, and they were prepared to release me. It was almost as though the decision was being taken from my hands and I resented it, but I agreed to play because I had never played against the All Blacks (and at that stage there was no guarantee the chance would come again) and because it would be fun to play in such a match with Tony on the other wing.

When all is said and done, though, there remains a certain prestige attached to the Barbarian name and if you are offered five days in Rome in May, when you have no family ties, you are unlikely to turn it down. Again I enjoyed the company of the players; I shared a room with Keith Robertson, the Scottish wing, and got to know him well, and inside us we had John Rutherford (at centre) and Malcolm Dacey. But even there we were obliged to follow a predetermined social calendar whereas most of us would have enjoyed exploring the city for ourselves. On our second night we were due for an evening at a pasta restaurant but when assembly time came four people were missing and, to the consternation of the club officials, we started off late for the function. However, the coach had hardly started off when four shambling figures came into view, having had a very sociable day by the look of it. They received a very stern dressing-down on the pavement from Rex Willis, the former Wales scrum-half who is on the Baa-baas committee, while the rest of us hurled abuse from the coach. I did get away on the odd occasion, to see the Colosseum in the company of Jean-Charles Orso, the French lock from Nice; Orso speaks good English and we were able to introduce him, after the game, to the pleasures of traditional British rugby pastimes like 'fizz-buzz', one of the many silly games played in pubs and bars by generations of rugby players. Several of the party were well on the way to enjoying themselves and, doubtless out of courtesy to Orso, we tried to play fizz-buzz in French and then silent fizz-buzz, which utterly baffled one West Country forward in the company!

7

Flying high – and low

One of the enduring strands of Rory's life has been his ambition to succeed in his RAF career, in particular to fly fast jets, the single-seat aircraft which represent the main strike force of the modern air force. The combination of demands made by the service and by his sport has not been easy to accommodate; it is a recurring theme for all internationals that in order to do well in their sport, they must probably concede something in their business and domestic lives – place their reliance on already overburdened colleagues, miss out on promotion, retake important examinations. That, of course, is their choice but there is something more at stake when you know that your country is investing something approaching £3 million in you so that, if the time should ever come to defend your country's interests, you should be capable of doing so effectively.

Sir Michael Knight knows better than most what is required to combine success in the RAF with success in rugby union. As well as achieving high rank in the service he represented the RAF on the Rugby Football Union committee for fifteen years and watched the developing career of the fledgling Rory with more than ordinary interest.

'It has been very difficult for Rory and the Royal Air Force to get this balance right. He is trying to do two things, each of which demands a great deal of effort and neither of which you can leave off for a long period of time and come straight back to.

You certainly can't do that with flying. Non-continuity is really very bad. Rory has had to work very hard indeed to fit these two things in. The RAF has helped him do that; there have been no special favours but we have recognised that here we have an international sportsman and, both for the game itself and for the Royal Air Force, we were keen to give him every opportunity to develop his talents on the rugby field. The three services operate *differently in this respect: the Royal Navy have the problem of shore and ship tours; the Army still operate the regimental system and the Regiment Commander can have the final say on the destiny of any of his young people. Will Carling might have stayed in the Army had he not fallen foul of the system which said that he should concentrate on other things rather than rugby.*

I don't think having an international sportsman on the strength does the service any harm in terms of recruitment. We have had those who haven't been as loyal to air force rugby as Rory has been; on the other side we have our shining examples such as Leighton Jenkins, Peter Larter, Jeff Young, all internationals who have put so much back into air force rugby. Rory has been exceptional in that regard. We have always ensured, it must be admitted, that our Royal Air Force Rugby Union committee was manned by people who are in reasonably influential positions and we normally have the Chief of the Air Staff as our president – which helps if you are writing to Station Commanders asking for some time off. If you are trying to run a station and you have certain goals to meet, certain standards you have to perform to, it's not going to help if some senior officer comes down and says, 'Oh, by the way, we want the following men off for four weeks in the summer, or eight weeks in the winter.' So it's done by give and take and I think most Station Commanders and their immediate juniors believe that sport is an integral part of service life, and it should be, and we're very proud of our internationals – not just in rugby but across the range of athletics, hockey and football.

It is more difficult when you get down to the sportsman's immediate boss. I have had young corporals say, 'Well, we know the Station Commander says yes but my Flight Sergeant is the guy who writes my report and I don't want rugby to hold me back.' It's a balance. In the days before the war part of being in the service was to play sport. Time was set aside for that, but those days are gone. What I would say is that there are not many in recent years who have played for the Royal Air Force who have not put back every bit that they've missed when they have been back at their stations. They travel huge distances to play and go back worn out and have to pick up the job.

I hope that Rory's commitment to rugby has not held back his service career. The choice he has made to retire represents probably his last chance to get back into the fast-jet stream. He has had, I believe, a very good run at getting a lot of experience under his belt,

*in the air, in jet aircraft, with a crew in Canberras – which are fairly
unforgiving aircraft. He has shown he can do that, he has made a
great success of his time on the squadron, he has become an
instrument rating examiner – which shows his competence as a
pilot – an authorising officer and has kept up the pace to a
remarkable degree. That shows his dedication.*

*Flying fast jet aircraft is a very demanding occupation. You really
have to give it 100 per cent. We always recognised, when Rory got
to the Tornado operational conversion unit, that had he gone on to
a front-line of quick reaction alert, and most of the Tornado force
was based in Germany and had he wished to play a full part as a
squadron member there would have been no question of him
getting back to play rugby for Leicester every week or having time
off to play for England. His international career would have
suffered, but Rory went flat out for the Tornado option and was
very disappointed not to make it at that time. When training air
crew it's a progressive operation, you make sure they can master
one layer before they move on to the next, and to become combat
air crew takes another 18 months to two years. You're talking
about five years' training and a cost of £2–3 million to get you into
that position. You can't afford to give people chances in the hope
they make it, and we didn't with Rory.'*

While England roughed it in New Zealand, losing to Auckland and
twice to New Zealand, I was flying Hawks from Valley where our
course developed an excellent spirit. Like any team sport, a good
feeling between the players can lift the side and it was the same in
Anglesey where, if anyone was a little down about some aspect of
flying, the rest gathered round to help him along. We were miles from
anywhere so we were thrown back very much on our own resources
but luckily it was the summer and it was easy to go swimming,
windsurfing or just to the beach. I even thought nothing of jumping
into the car and driving five hours to London because when there are
no responsibilities outside the job, the time spent on the motorway is
not a problem. Driving an hour to work and an hour back these days is
no hardship in comparison.

The Hawk was the advanced jet trainer, where the instructor sits
behind you; it can go supersonic, so long as it's 'clean' – not cluttered
up, that is, with pylons and bombs. The red and white aircraft used for
training is fondly known in the service as the 'Strawberry Ripple'; it
was faster, more manoeuvrable than the Provosts on which I had

trained before so the first part of the course was spent becoming accustomed to the Hawk's characteristics. The applied phase was low-level and formation flying, which took us all over the country, breaking the peace of many a rustic idyll on the way.

Again I started slowly but continuity and the assistance of one of the better instructors got me through the early part of the course and the applied phase went very well. At the end of the summer there was an overlap between the Valley course and my next course, at Chivenor near Barnstaple, which created a bit of a rush to finish the one before I started the other, flying the same aircraft but one belonging to Strike Command, camouflage paint and all – no longer the red L plates up, as it were. The firing buttons and the bomb-release triggers functioned, which underlined the ultimate purpose of the training, and because it carried a bomb load the general handling was slightly different, but the basic aim of the Chivenor course was learning how to fight, to fly for war.

I actually went to Chivenor without my wings, because I finished in Anglesey on the Friday and my new course began on the Monday. The presentation ceremony was arranged for later in the autumn so at Chivenor I was told to put up my wings anyway, otherwise it would look a bit odd swanning around without, apparently, having qualified – which, of course, I had. To earn your wings means having achieved a certain minimum standard in all phases of flying, but on top of that, you must have done well enough to proceed to the next stage of training; there have been situations where people may have passed the Valley course but not been deemed good enough for the next level. In such cases they would probably go on to flying Canberras or back to multi-engined training.

Not only did I have to fly under 'false colours', as it were, but when I arrived at Chivenor no one seemed to know I was coming. I had packed the MG Metro full of my gear and driven down from Anglesey to Somerset, which is a lovely part of the world, and met up with a couple of friends who had been at Valley. But coming into the classroom on the Monday morning there was no sign of the pilot's notes, flight reference cards and other books which would normally be laid out under my name. 'Maybe there's something they haven't told me,' I thought, but it was a bit embarrassing – not to say unnerving –so I had to sort it out before ground school could get under way.

Two weeks later I was back at Valley for the passing-out ceremony and presentation of my wings, packing all my No 1 uniform into the cockpit of the aircraft in which I hitched a ride. The family drove over from Barnard Castle, arriving the day after the squadron party during which we laid on a cabaret act, eight of us playing kazoos and miming the Glenn Miller hit 'In the Mood'. It also gave us the opportunity to do character assassinations of people in the squadron with a series of humorous sketches – which seemed to go down quite well. The Flight Commander distributed presents appropriate to the individuals passing out – one of the guys who had once had to divert because of running low on fuel was given a petrol can, and I received a pair of psychedelic sunglasses so that no one would recognise me!

When my mother and the family arrived it was my first opportunity to show her something of the life of a pilot, which she had never had the opportunity to see before. I took her down to the airfield where they were night flying and we just sat and watched the aircraft coming in; they were doing what we call 'rollers', flying in, touching down and taking off straight away which is like a series of practice landings. Mum couldn't quite understand what they were up to but the main part of the weekend for her was the next day, the presentations, when Sir Michael Knight had managed to organise matters so that he was the Presenting Officer – which was very thoughtful on his part since it neatly linked my service life and the rugby.

Two courses, about 14 people, were passing out and on top of receiving our wings there were presentations for best pilot, best ground school, aerobatics and the like. I was fortunate enough to receive the aerobatics award, which involves precision flying and co-ordination of a fairly high level, so there were stifled giggles among my fellow pilots when I marched up to the presenting platform and got it wrong. Got the marching wrong, that is; when you march, hands and legs are supposed to do the opposite. When they do the same we call it 'tick-tocking' and it's very unmilitary and not very co-ordinated. As soon as you start you know if you are doing it but it's almost impossible to get out of it. It was only a five-yard walk to the platform but there was an embarrassment factor of ten!

The officers' mess at Valley has a beautiful view and we had been able to get the Red Arrows to do a fly-past in celebration of our graduation. Every passing-out group spends its last fortnight ringing round other squadrons, even as far afield as Germany, trying to make sure of a fly-past in its honour; the weather wasn't brilliant but the Red Arrows were on their way back from the north and did the honours for us, which was superb entertainment for everyone. We also persuaded four F-111s and four Tornados to come and practise airfield attacks, so the afternoon amounted to a private air show for all the guests even though there was a limit to what they could do; but there could have been no better illustration to our families, or ourselves for that matter, of what we had earned our wings for.

The proud parents departed after that, leaving the graduates to their happy hour, and we had one last sketch up our sleeves. Six of us had planned a Red Arrows show of our own: we got hold of a ghetto-blaster and set it on the patio wall outside the officers' mess, booming out Wagner's 'Ride of the Valkyries', while we lined up in echelon, arms outstretched, with me leading. I was carrying a day–night flare like those used on survival courses – when you ditch you have a double-ended flare which glows at night-time and gives off smoke in the day. We had used the night end two days earlier, to welcome back our Flight Commander by creating a trip switch so that when he drove into his garage he set off the flare. You really need ingenuity to be a pilot! Now we used the smoke end as we did our precision flying at ground level, even down to a roll where two of us came running on a crisscross and went head over heels before streaking off again. The finale was the fly-past as I ripped the top off the flare and we went 'smoking' towards the crowd line before the command of 'Break', at which we all broke off singly, surrounded the Flight Commander and threw him in the lake near the mess. It was quite a good night after that!

Still, all good things come to an end and that was emphasised on the Monday when I came to fly back down to Chivenor. All my previous experience had been with an instructor; now I flew south with a friend, both of us with the same flying experience, no one to tell us how to go. It was a symbolic moment; perhaps we both realised the additional responsibility we had, that our superiors acknowledged we were capable of looking after ourselves and our rather expensive equipment.

Chivenor was another 65-hour course, much of it comprising close-formation flying or tactical formation, and weaponeering – that is, use of the weapons with which the aircraft is equipped, learning how to use the sights and lining up your opponent. Although much of the work conforms to a set pattern, aerial combat doesn't leave too much time for thinking so the confidence you have in your ability to handle the aircraft is taken for granted; this course added another layer to that confidence. At high level the flying is comparatively easy; at low level there is the additional factor to be taken into account of proximity to the ground, which increases the risk of collision so there are certain basic rules of formation flying to be taken in – ground rules of the most literal kind in this case.

There was a lot to take in and one day I took off with another Hawk in company, in fairly gloomy conditions with cloud at 1000 feet; adding to the difficulties, the radar went down so we had to work out exactly where we were with the instruments. I was leading for the first time – I had always been someone else's wingman before – and I had certainly never led for a self-positioned recovery. I elected to approach the airfield from ten miles out at 2000 feet, all checks done, in formation with my colleague, and if you have ever heard the expression 'maxed out', that's what happened to me on that trip; in simple terms there was only so much my brain could absorb.

I was concerned with my flying, worrying about my No 2 on my wing, trying to control my height and keep the aircraft steady, trying to work out where I was in relation to the runway, and it wasn't coming together. I was going up and down before we eventually landed, with an instructor in the back, whose sympathy for students seemed less than total, urging me to 'sort myself out' – which didn't help. A self-position job, in cloud, is not easy and I had never done one before; at that stage I couldn't cope with it so I went 'on review', which is a stage nearer being axed from the course. But, from that day on, not a thing went wrong. Remaining sorties went brilliantly; it was as though, having emerged from a crisis, I had found the answer and I was one of the few people at the end of the course who got a 'successfully off review' certificate – which said that 'despite the attempts of all at 63 Squadron you have successfully passed the course while being on review'. It was a thoroughly enjoyable course, starting to use your brain in the three-dimensional sense in fights. It concluded with a practice bomb run on two targets in Wales, one a level attack, the other a diving attack while trying to avoid the attentions of an 'enemy' fighter who is trying to 'bounce' you. When you spot the bounce you go into defensive manoeuvres yourself and turn towards him; having negated the threat you have to resume your route towards the targets before turning for home, keeping an eye on the fuel gauge at all times. It is designed as a 50-minute sortie which, taken together with the two-hour briefing time you are allowed before take-off, leaves you absolutely knackered.

At the end of the course you discover which aircraft you will go on to. There were six options – Harrier, Jaguar, Tornado GR1, Tornado F3, Buccaneer and the Phantom. An interview with the Flight Commander is one way of finding out your posting, but we chose a less formal way – the Beer Hunter! Six cans of beer were placed in a tub, each labelled with an aircraft type, and the can with your posting on it was well shaken. You chose a can blindly and, holding it to your head, opened it. If you were sprayed, then that was your posting. Mine turned out to be the Tornado GR1 at Cottesmore. I had been hoping for Jaguars and, on my low-level flying marks, might have earned it but the instrument flying and general handling not having gone so well I couldn't argue against being given a two-seater aircraft. The point was that I was flying fast jets.

The rugby, meanwhile, had been on hold. I missed the first half of Leicester's season, though I was able to play for Yorkshire and the North, making trips from Barnstaple to Brize Norton, where I stayed with Ian Goslin, the RAF centre, overnight before driving on the Saturday to wherever the game was. Then it was back to Ian's on the Saturday night and home to Chivenor on the Sunday. My first match of the season in Leicester colours was that against the Barbarians at the end of December – two days before the announcement of England's team to play Wales. It coincided with a decent period of leave before I was due for my refresher course on Tornados at Cottesmore, which was made more enjoyable when confirmation of the team came through; I had missed the summer tour and, there being no autumn international, my rugby had been comparatively limited, but I resumed in a team including two newcomers, Graham Robbins, the Coventry No 8, and Simon Halliday, then Bath's centre.

At that stage I was enjoying a bit of freedom, spending a lot of time with friends in London – not that I'm a great one for the high life. You wouldn't have found me in discos or night clubs every evening but I like relaxing with friends, just chatting in a pub. I don't get much pleasure out of noisy parties, loud music, a smoky atmosphere and though I can dance, it's not something I would do at the drop of a hat.

Or the drop of a goal, for that matter, which turned out to be the difference between England and Wales. As was the case those days we went into the match with no distinct idea that we would win, unlike the teams which have played under Will Carling in the last three years. In 1986 we knew we would always have our work cut out against France but we always gave ourselves a chance against the other three home unions – not because we believed the standard to be so much poorer but because of our limited knowledge and confidence in ourselves as individuals and as a team. Now, we understand where we want to play the game, how we want to play the game. Then, most of us left matters to the acknowledged decision-makers and hoped all would be well on the afternoon; there was no consistency in our standard of performance, no clear idea of the likely progress of the 80 minutes. Taking on Wales at Twickenham we felt we had a prospect, and I suppose it illustrates my point that the game see-sawed a lot, Wales leading midway through the first half, England ahead at half-time, Wales back in front at three-quarter time and Rob dropping the goal which won the game three minutes into injury time, to go with his six penalties.

Rob was flavour of the month then; he appeared on the *Wogan* show on television, and couldn't have imagined the harsh criticism he was to come in for in the next two years. We celebrated, of course, though there was little enough for me to celebrate a week later because, for about the only time in my career, I suffered a mid-season injury. Playing a cup match for Leicester against Coventry I went for a pass from Les Cusworth which went straight through my hands, hit my head and as I turned to retrieve the ball, I twisted my ankle. With treatment it might not have mattered – on tour in 1988 when I did something similar, Kevin Murphy, the England physiotherapist, had me playing again in ten days – but I was travelling up and down and three weeks later it still had not improved enough for me to pass a fitness test. Both Huw Davies and I turned up at Twickenham to be assessed by Don Rutherford, the Rugby Football Union's technical director; Huw passed and I failed.

So for the only time I had to pull out of an international, which gave Mickey Harrison his first championship cap against Scotland at Murrayfield. I was very disappointed but, with hindsight, it was not a bad game to miss and I was delighted for Mickey, although events moved so swiftly I didn't have the chance to congratulate him. I don't know that the possibility registered that I might not get back; it was merely a temporary setback and the selection meant that England were once again fielding two specialist right wings anyway. That weekend I was staying with friends in Bicester and dived into Oxford on the Saturday to get a radio for my new car; I saw bits of the game on television in shop windows and very quickly gathered that things were not going England's way. But it was not until I arrived back at Bicester that I was told they had lost 33–6 and I couldn't believe it.

I watched the highlights on *Rugby Special* the next day and it appeared as though everything went Scotland's way, every bounce, every kick. Having said that, it obviously wasn't England's best performance of all time so perhaps it was no surprise that there were eight changes made for the next game, against Ireland; although it was bad luck for Simon Smith, my return meant Mickey moved from left to right wing and Leicester had another player included when Dean Richards was called up for his first cap at No 8. Leicester have never had a great history of pushing their own players before they believe they are ready but in Deano's case he might have been played earlier than he was; everyone knows his strengths now, but he had been doing great things for Leicester.

He did great things against the Irish too: two tries in your first match isn't bad. The game nearly didn't take place because the weather was so poor. When we met for training we spent some time at Twickenham and at one stage I helped answer the flood of calls from the public, asking whether the game would go ahead. On the Saturday there were mounds of snow at each end and thermal underwear, courtesy of Nike, was the order of the day. It nearly started with a bang for Mickey because he was over for a try in the first few minutes, only to be called back because the touch judge had spotted Steve Brain throwing a punch near halfway and Ireland were given a penalty instead. There weren't too many chances for the backs after that because the forwards took control and Deano got both his tries from pushovers – and narrowly missed a third, though we were given a penalty try instead. It's funny how times change. We got tremendous support from the crowd because we were scoring a lot of points (it finished 25–20) whereas now people are hypercritical; they want scores but they want them in style too.

Victory gave England the (then) unaccustomed luxury of two championship wins and a theoretical tilt at the title in the last match, against France; theory is all it was, though. A scoreline of 29–10 in Paris said everything. Late in the game I made 60 metres across field in an attempt to stop the fourth French try only to have the ball lobbed over my head and Philippe Sella purred over for the try. The season, though, was not quite over. Under other circumstances there would have been a British Lions tour to South Africa but the invitation to tour was withdrawn and instead there were two games to celebrate the centenary of the International Rugby Football Board, the first at Cardiff involving a Lions XV against the overseas unions, the second at Twickenham pitting the Five Nations against the rest.

My availability for those depended upon RAF duties, because I had to present myself at North Luffenham for a change of flying gear to suit Tornados and decompression exercises which simulate the effect of flying at 40,000 feet. Having learned of the discomforts of oxygen debt and its effects upon the human body and brain, we were then wheeled down to Plymouth for combat survival and rescue training, which wasn't considered very popular since it began on Easter Monday. I don't think the organisers of the course had realised that it was Easter weekend. None the less, the service called and it was into escape/evasion work, learning how to make a tent out of a parachute, though most of it took place in the classroom or just outside. We were also taken out to sea and 'dumped' from a boat, so that we could accustom ourselves to the idea of baling out over water. I had done exercises in a swimming pool but never at sea, which involves the pilot and his one-man dinghy and bringing the two together – which is not as easy as it sounds when you have to wriggle your way in, Mae West and all, and make sure you're totally protected from the water.

You may take my word for it that the experience reduces your perception: you can see little at wave level and it's very easy to become seasick. As it happens, although it was April the water was not too cold and it was a sunny day so once I was inside my canopy in the dinghy, it was quite snug – allowing for having to bale every now and again. At night-time in a rough sea it must be horrifying but at the time it quickly becomes boring as you wait for an hour or so for a helicopter to arrive and pick you up. I must have dozed off because the next thing I knew there were voices and I was being told to climb aboard a Gemini dinghy – no helicopter because the message to the search and rescue squadron asking them to rendezvous with eight souls in the Channel had been treated as a spoof! It arrived on Easter Monday and, they thought, no one works on a Bank Holiday Monday.

So much for combat survival. My return to the Midlands was via London because the RAF were playing so I missed the first day of ground school, when the aircrew from West Germany and Italy arrived. It was a four-week ground school and by this time I had been invited to play in the IRFB matches, which involved missing the second week of the course. The hope was that I could pick up what I had missed in the third and fourth weeks, when the work is not so intensive, so I travelled to Cardiff to play for the Lions against all these big names from overseas, Serge Blanco, Andrew Slack, Nick Farr-Jones and Murray Mexted among them. It was a wet evening and the Lions lost 15–7 in a far from memorable game; so we moved to Twickenham, amid an argument over who should play on the wing for the Five Nations, the French being very annoyed when Patrick Estève was omitted. As it was they had four representatives, Blanco, Sella, Laurent Rodriguez and Jean Condom, and I was surprised to find how psyched up they were for the game, punching each other and generally winding each other up. In the light of England's most recent experience in Paris, with two Frenchmen being sent off in the closing stages, perhaps they need a cooler approach before the match.

As far as I was concerned it was a big game but it was a show game – one of those occasions when you are thrown together as a side without much time to prepare. It was labelled as the northern hemisphere against the south, which I didn't really like, and the players from down under displayed an arrogance towards British rugby that wasn't very enjoyable. Whether or not it was justified is neither here nor there. It was interesting playing in a Five Nations side although getting an understanding with the French contingent wasn't easy, and I don't see there being much room for it in the northern-hemisphere season. The opposing left wing was Carel du Plessis, the South African who scored such a good try during the game; he seemed a nice guy to talk to but he didn't look the classic wing since he had a stocky frame and a strange running action, not your out-and-out speed merchant. For all that he took his try well enough, but the man who took the eye again was Danie Gerber, in the centre, who scored two tries in their 32–13 win.

So the season slipped away and, with no tour in the summer, I was left to concentrate upon my flying. I went straight back to Cottesmore and ground school but I found it hard; it wasn't easy for me to get to grips with the academic requirements of this electric bomber. I had been trying to work through some manuals during my week away but good intentions aren't enough if you don't fully grasp the demands of the systems involved. I had one-to-one tuition and started doing simulator rides and the course wasn't going too badly, but I missed the pass mark of 70 per cent by 1 per cent. So I had to retake the examination and it became steadily worse. However, there had been sufficiently encouraging facets of it for the authorities to have a debate about my immediate future and put me through the examination with an instructor present, so that both he and I could appreciate where exactly the trouble lay.

They must have felt that it was worth persisting so we began the flying school, in my case with a German instructor because it was a tri-national Tornado training course. However, not all the Germans were qualified flying instructors, while all the British were, and though training began well enough and I got on with my instructor, he obviously felt I should be left to my own devices for much of the time. A couple of instrument flights showed me in an undistinguished light and a formation flight in which I was the leader was less than brilliant. The transition from Hawks to front-line jets, and the changes in flying approach, were not adequate; the teaching wasn't getting through and I was struggling. In one sortie I flew several bad approaches; I couldn't understand what was going wrong, and it wasn't easy to talk it through with my instructor in the crew room. I asked for more trips and was given them, but I failed my first instrument rating test, even though the basic handling was reasonably good. That forced the squadron to put me on review; I was given more simulator rides and a British instructor and this time I made progress and got a very good mark on my tests. The next step was to get my general handling improved before flying with a student navigator but the initial sorties received, as they say, mixed reviews. I failed the second sortie and the next day I went to see the Station Commander who told me he had started to convene a suspension board to examine my case. That came as a complete shock; suddenly I was going from a reasonably average pilot straight into reverse at a rapid rate of knots, having never failed a test sortie until that stage.

That afternoon I found my entire flying career under review. At first I had thought it was a preliminary discussion about what would happen when the board of suspension convened; then it clicked that the board was in being and that I was fighting for my place on the Tornado course. From trying to explain politely that I felt I had not received proper tuition in making the transition to the Tornado, I found I needed to be somewhat more forceful, to try to claw back the ground it appeared I had lost. The discussion continued, increasingly desperate on my part, before I left the room and was then summoned back in; I think the decision had already been reached but I was told my instrument flying was not up to standard and that the board would recommend my suspension from flying the Tornado.

It was the collapse of my immediate world. In the space of 24 hours I had gone from what I thought was a gradually improving position to being chopped from the course at which I was so keen to do well. The Station Commander agreed with the board's findings and advised me to compose a letter accepting those findings and stating my preferred option — though at that stage I had given no thought at all to what I wanted to do if I couldn't fly fast jets. His recommendation was that I request a transfer to fly Hercules, the heavy-duty transport aircraft, which is what I did, but I could have wept — and nearly did. I hung around the station waiting for the course to end and to receive my next posting, miserable as sin; two weeks later one of the crews from my course was killed in an accident when their Tornado flew into the ground in Wales. I heard about it in the small hours of a June morning when one of the other course members staggered into my room, fairly drunk, and said that two of the boys had crashed. To say that it cast a gloom over all of us is grossly to understate the case, but we had all been aware, for a long time, of the risks involved in our chosen career. The accident served to emphasise those risks. The tradition in the RAF, when you lose a member of the 'family' in this way, is to drink all night on his bar book and then throw it away – all debts written off – and that is what we did.

Personally it brought me down to earth and put my woes into grim perspective. It was as well, though, that there was a break of a month between courses which enabled me to take a three-week holiday in Malaysia. I had either been playing rugby or concentrating on flying and, for the first time in a long while, I had both the time and the funds to go abroad without affecting either. Before I did so, however, my next posting arrived and to my great joy I discovered that I had been sent to fly Canberras. I think they had not occurred to me because in the fast-jet world, the Canberra – a twin-engined, medium-range bomber – is seen as the old man's aircraft, the workhorse of the jets. The Morris Minor, if you like. But upon reflection they were by far the best option, which should have occurred to me because a friend had been posted to them; had I gone to Hercules the road back to fast jets would have been very long, perhaps up to ten years, whereas the Canberra reduced that period by nearly half. All of a sudden the future didn't look so bleak and the course dates even fitted with my immediate plans.

I had come to terms with the blow to my career. Looking back I suppose I accepted what I was told without making the fight that I understand some people have done, by writing to higher authority to complain, but if I had done so and the verdict had been changed, I doubt if my international rugby career would have been sustained in the way that it was. Moreover my domestic life took a very definite turn for the better. Into each life some sun must shine, I suppose.

As it happened, the last event of the course was the traditional summer ball after which the rest of the course would prepare to depart for Honington. However, several old friends from Valley were making up a party to attend the ball, which lifted my spirits, and we all arrived at the officers' mess prepared for a pleasant, relaxed evening with something of a reunion about it. During the evening my eye was caught by a Flying Officer who had arrived at Cottesmore at much the same time as I had. Wendy Blanshard was working in the air-traffic branch after four months in the Falklands and, as I passed with a tray of drinks, I asked her for a dance. Later, I summoned the nerve to follow it up and that was the start of a relationship which very quickly ripened into friendship.

Wendy comes from Immingham, in South Humberside, and she came to understand very quickly how romantically inclined I am since, two days after we met, I took myself off for three weeks on holiday. She has never forgiven me for that! I sent her two postcards from Malaysia, in one of which I mispelled her surname, but the day after I arrived home I went round to see her and she seemed pleased to see me. Our friendship developed until I was dispatched to Wyton in Cambridgeshire for an eight-day ground school on Canberras, which I passed with flying colours (compared with the Tornado ground school). I started flying training on the Operational Conversion Unit in July; that took me to 360 Squadron, also based at Wyton, which I joined in November 1986. Since that was only 35 miles away from Cottesmore my love life was not irretrievably blighted either, although my Fiat Strada 130TC Abarth was eating up the petrol. In December I proposed to Wendy. You could argue that 1986 had not been an entirely bad year. On the one hand I had failed my chosen course. On the other I had met my future wife and had received a posting which meant we could see each other relatively easily which, if I had continued on the Tornado, would not have been the case, and I could continue playing rugby.

8

World Cup woes

In a few short years the concept of a world cup for rugby union has become accepted very readily. Coming as it did in 1987 it complemented the competitive attitudes inbred in the southern-hemisphere countries and coincided with the drive towards a league structure in England. International players in England had often expressed a yearning for such a tournament – rugby's own Olympics, as it were – only to be told by the game's administrators that there was neither the room nor the demand for it. However, pressure from the southern hemisphere told: Australia and New Zealand carried out a feasibility study and persuaded their colleagues on the International Rugby Football Board to accept their findings. France, who had mooted the idea several years earlier, needed little convincing anyway.

The natural venue for the inaugural World Cup would have been Britain, where the stadia, the crowds and the finance existed. Lack of enthusiasm, however, among the administrators of the four home unions ensured that the tournament took place on a shared basis in New Zealand and Australia. Uncertain about what was about to hit them, except that it was likely to be harder, faster and fitter than their own material, the Rugby Football Union put in motion the fitness drive which helped produce a completely new breed of rugby player five years later. Athleticism became the buzz word and the concept of team management, as opposed to the traditional chairman of selectors and his panel, entered English thinking. Tom McNab, who helped prepare the English squad, discovered that Rory possessed, in his words, 'the finest natural physique I've come across, which is remarkable considering he's not even a trained athlete'. Rory's tests suggested he rated comparison with Daley Thompson, then the Olympic decathlon champion. 'Even the most dedicated of men, like Alan Wells, don't have such thigh muscle development,' McNab gloated.

The two games in 1986 to celebrate the International Board's centenary gave a hint of what was to come in the World Cup. A further hint was dropped at the inaugural Sydney Sevens that same year, when England sent a somewhat disorganised squad and paid the penalty, losing to Australia and Spain and struggling to beat the Netherlands. That same summer England selected a squad of players and gave them personal training schedules, so as to try to close the gap in preparation between their own players and what they knew of the southern hemisphere – where Australia had just won a series in New Zealand for the first time and could rightly be acclaimed world champions in the continued absence from international competition of South Africa.

The idea of a World Cup was enormously appealing. The main distinction, in my mind, between a tournament and a tour is the variety on offer. On tour you prepare yourself to play one country twice, which is a challenge, but to play a series of international matches is completely different. Obviously the difference in quality is taken into account; we very soon realised when the pools were known that the primary match was the one against Australia, with the USA and Japan making up the numbers in that pool, which was the only one to be played in Australia. The other three pools were all played in New Zealand.

There was added spice for me because I had missed the two England tours made during my time as an international player, to South Africa in 1984 and New Zealand in 1985. At the time that had not been a matter for great regret; I knew of the logistical problems and accepted them and concentrated on my flying duties. I would have enjoyed touring but it just wasn't possible at that particular time. But the chance to play against so many other international teams was not to be missed; my experience then was limited to the home unions, France, Romania and Australia, with Japan coming into England in the autumn of 1986. As England players we knew we were a mid-table side in Five Nations championship terms but the chance to measure ourselves against the best in the world and determine a true international ranking would have appealed to any sportsman.

The first hint of a new regime came when the squad gathered at Bisham Abbey in August of 1986 and we were introduced to Tom McNab. Tom has enjoyed a distinguished career in various fields, as author, film scriptwriter but more particularly as an athletics coach, both to individuals and to the national squad. It was his job to introduce to a bunch of rugby players the sort of fitness concepts other sports had long taken for granted but which rugby had yet to learn –

and about which some of its practitioners were somewhat sceptical. Nowadays we take them for granted but so much of it was new then and it reflects credit on Mike Weston, then the chairman of selectors, and Martin Green, the coach, that they brought in 'outside' help.

The England team was still evolving from the players who had won the 1980 grand slam towards the players who finally won the 1991 grand slam, but it was very much betwixt and between, neither fish nor fowl during the 1986–87 season. Though the 1980 grand slammers had gone, many of their ilk remained, brought up in a traditional approach to rugby. I was one of a newer breed, perhaps more open-minded about trying new ideas. Tom laid it on the line from the first day. He had studied the relative amounts of time in which forwards pushed and shoved and rucked and mauled, and that backs spent in sprints of varying distances, and he told all of us what would be required to make ourselves better players. We were introduced to the idea of lifting weights and were told that Judy Oakes, the international shot putter, would be coming to teach us how to lift them. That in itself came as a surprise, that a woman would be teaching men how to lift weights, but one incident brought home to us how much we had to learn. One of the squad was having problems with his lift and Mickey Harrison had a little chuckle to himself, at which stage Judy rounded on him and told him he'd be better off at home if he wasn't prepared to learn. It wasn't easy for her, trying to teach new techniques to a squad rather than to individuals, but it was all part of opening our minds to a different way of doing things.

Earlier in the year, when I had been fitness tested before withdrawing from the match with Scotland, it had consisted of a few jogs and sprints up and down the corridor at Twickenham. Now we were learning about power lifts, distance running and the like; I found a lot of it coming quite easily, because I have a lot of natural power in my legs which helps with the explosive throwing techniques such as putting the shot. I managed to beat Steve Bainbridge, the lock from Newcastle, in some of the disciplines and he was not amused because he had a background as a decathlete and felt that he knew a bit more about the new territory we were heading for than some of his forward colleagues.

At the same time Tom produced diet sheets, which brought very definite mutterings of discontent. The sheets told us which foods were good for us and which were not; nothing was forced upon us, nor is it today although we know that the night before an international, chicken will be on the menu because the white meat is more easily digested. It's not the best-kept secret that my own diet is fairly basic – fast foods and chocolate feature – but when we're together as a squad now there will be a lot of rice and pasta available to build up the carbohydrates.

Most of us realised that the new approach would make greater demands upon our time. I had just started going out with Wendy and little did she know what she was letting herself in for over the next six years. But that was the birth of everything that followed, the raw beginning which came to be fine-tuned by the management team created by Geoff Cooke. As it was, for the first match of that season, against the touring Japanese, the preparation tended to revolve entirely around the back row; there was little continuity, bringing backs and forwards together, and anyone who remembers that game may recall there was little enough in it until the final quarter when we pulled away, mainly because of our physical advantage and the confidence we derived from getting ahead on the scoreboard.

For the first time, too, we went to Portugal for warm-weather training in October. The idea was to prepare on hard grounds over an extended weekend, both for the Five Nations championship and for the conditions expected during the World Cup in Australia. While we were there Mike Weston was in Australia with the other World Cup managers, making sure all the arrangements were up to scratch. Everyone, in a sense, was rushing around preparing for something they had never experienced before; when you remember that the 1991 World Cup was the climax of two years of preparation, with tours planned around it, it is not entirely surprising that not all the steps England took in 1987 came off. Certainly it was not the most brilliant of championship campaigns and you could never have accused the squad of leaving for Australia with confidence bubbling.

Perhaps the writing was on the wall with the England trial that season, when England beat the Rest by only one point, 10–9, which clearly suggested that getting the right mix would not be easy. It was the season when northern rugby came into its own; Mickey Harrison became captain of Yorkshire, the North and, ultimately, England after never captaining a side before. The North won the divisional championship with an outstanding win over London and a young lad called Will Carling, whom not many of us knew anything about, emerged from Durham University to play centre for the Rest.

Will's time was still to come, though. The centres picked against Scotland were Jamie Salmon and Kevin Simms, only for freezing weather to force a postponement. By the time we played our first championship match, in early February, we had lost Dean Richards with a knee injury which kept him out of the championship until the final match. Maybe the memory bank chooses not to retain matches such as that against Ireland in Dublin that season. All I can remember about it is visiting Lansdowne Road after training on the Friday and John Hall, who was carrying a ball, deciding to try an Australian Rules-style bounce-off in the middle of the pitch. He smashed the ball down so hard it came straight back and hit him in the face, and 20 other players cracked up laughing. We didn't have much to laugh about after that; when we arrived at the ground the next day for the game it was a lovely afternoon, but when we emerged changed for the team photograph the rain was hammering down. We won scarcely any ball and what we did win was difficult to handle – so was Phil Matthews when he scored the second of Ireland's three tries. I caught him with a good tackle and lifted him off the ground but he slid through my hands over the top and touched down; Ireland won 17–0, which says enough about the game from our point of view.

Certainly we all felt considerably better after the next game, against France, even though we lost. Wade Dooley and Steve Bainbridge, who had missed the Irish game, came together in the second row and the experiment began of playing Peter Winterbottom and Gary Rees as left- and right-hand flankers in the back row. You could argue that we might have won but for an interception try from Philippe Sella but, at 19–15, it was sufficiently close to the best team in the championship to have offered us encouragement.

Any such feelings were promptly erased by the next match, the infamous brawl in Cardiff which resulted in four England players being suspended for one match. It was my second visit there and of course the gap since England had last won there was getting wider all the time, but there was no reason for this match to have gone the way it did. The England–Wales game was still the major encounter among the four home unions in those days. *The* big match, and Richard Hill, who was captain that season, became pretty worked up beforehand. In a short time he had become well known for his pre-match team talks – after one of them Marcus Rose asked if he would mind not swearing quite so much – but perhaps he felt this one more, both because it was Wales we were playing and because in his other two matches as captain, both had been lost. Richard's speech in the changing room will live in the memory of all who were there, although I have to say that what is said at that stage of the preparation has very little effect on me. I try to focus in on what I have to do during the match and, now that we have had such a settled routine under Will Carling's leadership, that has become much easier.

To be honest, I cannot remember that game as being unduly dirty, apart from the one incident at the start when the two Welshmen, Steve Sutton and Phil Davies, were injured. If you ask me what match sends shivers down my spine I would say it was my first game at Lansdowne Road, when there were green shirts leaping into rucks from everywhere. The Welsh game was hard but no harder than some others I have played in. Divorced from the action by being out on the wing, anything I remember was gleaned from television afterwards; it's very rare for me to see fights in a line-out because I'm looking for the ball. It's television that focuses the eye on incidents which happen off the ball. The major impression left on me was by the Welsh pack as I tried to collect a kick into the corner from Jonathan Davies and their forwards came rumbling over me for Stuart Evans to score the only try of the match, which they won 19–12.

To cap a wonderful day we had just got back to the Crest Hotel when the fire alarm went off and we all went out to stand in the drizzle and reflect on life's injustices. It was the first time Wendy had come with me to Cardiff and we were all left with a sour taste in the mouth; it was not a good night. We drove back home on Sunday but in one sense it was the calm before the storm. There were demands in the press for heads to roll and ten days later the Rugby Football Union suspended Gareth Chilcott, Graham Dawe, Wade Dooley and Richard Hill from selection for the final championship game, against Scotland; the really strange thing, to my mind, was that not a Welshman seemed to have been involved. From what I had seen there had been blows struck from their side and it is seldom the case that all the provocation is coming from one side. But they had won so they were quite happy, whereas England were looking for scapegoats.

As players we had had little chance to discuss the match. There was not the same camaraderie as there is now, in any case, but today, under the normal rota of championships matches, we would be together again for training the following weekend. In 1987 we did not come together again until two days before the next match. We had all shot off in our different directions and in fact, that year we did not come together again for another month because the Scottish match was moved to April. It seemed to me as though the RFU was determined to make a stand, which seemed rather one-sided, since the Welsh did nothing. It left the English selectors in a difficult position too: one more match to go before the inaugural World Cup and a major upheaval in team building. Indeed, when the team to play Scotland was announced there were eight changes of one sort or another and Mickey Harrison, who started the season having captained no one, added the captaincy of England to his county and divisional honours.

One significant newcomer was at hooker, where Brian Moore appeared for the first time, with Paul Rendall as his loose head. Rob Andrew was dropped and we had new half-backs in Richard Harding and Peter Williams, and Simon Halliday returned, while Peter Winterbottom lost his place in the back row to John Hall, who moved from No 8 to allow Dean Richards to return. It was the last opportunity to salvage something from what had become a disastrous season; since then the Scottish match has come to assume an even greater status because of the consistency they have achieved, aided by the moves that started after the first World Cup, when they began looking elsewhere for players, outside Scotland. They uncovered people like David Sole, Damian Cronin and Chris Gray, not all of whom were Scottish by upbringing and most of whose rugby had been played in England; in some senses they have become more 'Scottish' than those who were brought up in Scotland. The Bath lads were quite amused as David's accent changed from English to Scottish!

When I first played against Scotland it was one of the matches I most enjoyed because there wasn't the nationalistic fervour that the Welsh game brought out (win or lose the Irish are always good to play against). I got on really well with people like Roger Baird, John Rutherford and Peter Steven who were in the Scottish side when I began, but over the last two or three years the atmosphere has changed and not for the better. As individuals it's fine but put two or three of them together and they become far more aggressive in their nationalism, while the Welsh, as their record has declined, have become less strident. That appears to be one of the side effects of success.

That year Scotland were going for the triple crown but they foundered as much on Marcus Rose at full-back as on anyone else. Marcus scored 17 points in our 21–12 win and suddenly the world was a little brighter and events began to move somewhat faster; a few days later England's World Cup squad was announced, which was a special moment for me since it was my first overseas trip with the senior side. That same week Mickey Harrison and I joined forces with Rob Andrew and Peter Winterbottom to help Yorkshire win the county championship against Middlesex at Twickenham, and then we were off to Portugal on another extended training camp.

Three weeks later we assembled again and suddenly the World Cup was no longer a vague dream on the horizon, it was staring us in the face. We met for kitting out and had a run at Twickenham to make sure everyone was fit; tea and biscuits in the committee room with wives and girlfriends and then we were on our way. Even for those who had been to Australia before, which I had not, it was an adventure and no sooner had we arrived in Sydney than it was north to Brisbane where Australia were playing a warm-up game against South Korea. Immediately we had checked into our hotel in mid-morning there was time only for a brief lunch before we climbed into playing kit and back on to the coach for a training run. Not that it was quite so easy for a somewhat jet-lagged party; even for me it was the longest trip I had taken on an aircraft – four or five hours longer than travelling to Malaysia – and neither Rob nor I could resist lying down in the room we were sharing, only to waken with a start to the realisation that the coach would be leaving without us if we weren't careful.

It always takes a day or two to get the system working properly, by which time we were back in Sydney to prepare for our opening World Cup match, against Australia. The team was based in Rushcutters Bay, a nice enough part of Sydney, but the hotel really was poor, which was a shame because all the other arrangements seemed to work well enough and it was convenient having our training pitch just outside the hotel. It was a whole new experience, training every day, but we very quickly came to understand that the tournament was not quite the event we thought it was going to be; rugby union was very definitely the poor relation to rugby league and Australian Rules football and even up to the opening day of the World Cup, negotiations were going on over the television rights.

At least Rob had the benefit of knowing the local scene, because he had spent the previous summer in Sydney playing for Gordon, one of the first-division clubs. However, Orrell's Peter Williams was the first-choice fly-half and Rob had to occupy the replacements bench for the opening game and watch as England went down 19–6. The feeling was that we had done quite well, particularly since David Campese scored a try which should not have been allowed. But it gave us an idea of the standards we had to achieve and Peter Williams – Gobbler as he is known – brought off one of the best tackles I have ever seen when Peter Grigg, the Australian wing, blasted a way through Jamie Salmon and me only to be brought down by a perfect low tackle. Sadly it did not stop a try because Simon Poidevin picked up and scored, but Peter deserved better for his effort. Campo's score came when we were attacking out of defence and the ball went down in midfield, allowing them to kick through, and Campo collected, only for Peter to tackle him on the line and the ball went forward. It was another amazing effort to have reached the position to make the tackle and Peter went up hugely in my estimation for his work in that game. But Keith Lawrence, the referee, decided that Campo had touched down, which maybe he wouldn't have done if there had been better understanding between the referee and touch judges. But Lawrence, a New Zealander, had René Hourquet, a Frenchman, on the line and I don't believe there was any communication between them over the incident.

We were disappointed to have lost but we scored a good try in which Jonathan Webb played a part. He had come on for his first cap after Marcus Rose hit his head on the ground in Grigg's tackle and left the field concussed after only a few minutes. Webbie had a bang early in the game too, which helped account for the fact that he missed all his kicks apart from the one conversion; when we were back in the hotel that evening he went to his room because he wasn't feeling well and afterwards he had no recollection of the game at all. At one stage he wandered into my room and asked when the highlights would be on the television, an hour after we had both watched them.

Perhaps it was as well for him that the RFU had decided to give us a break after the first game. They felt it would prevent the daily routine becoming boring and we were whisked off to Hamilton Island, up on the Barrier Reef, which, whatever the reasoning behind it, was a fantastic break. There were players wandering around with their eyes popping, everything was so different and there were so many facilities available for recreation. The choice of restaurants, the beaches, the incredible warmth of the water, the jet ski-ing, it was brilliant. There were helicopter rides out to the Reef too, four at a time being dropped off at the pontoon, but the Reef itself was actually exposed when I was there and you could walk around on it. The next year, when England were in Australia and made a similar trip, we made a more extended visit by boat to the Reef but there was nothing visible until you got below sea level – either in it or under it in the glass-bottomed boat they use so that tourists can see the magical colours of the different corals.

All good things come to an end, though, and after four days we returned to Sydney to prepare for the match with Japan which had to be won if we were to stay in the tournament. The context was very different from the meeting with the Japanese at Twickenham the previous year; then we had just come together as a side whereas now we had been training together and had played a game together and, as it turned out, we were far too good for them. The 60–7 margin remains an England record. I scored two tries, neither of them particularly testing, and we had ten in all which was a healthy return and left us in good spirits for the final pool game, against the USA.

I was rested for that match, which gave Mark Bailey the chance of a game; I was a bit disappointed to miss an international, although I knew there was no question of being dropped. Occupying the bench was an unusual experience and I watched England win 34–6, a hard enough game even if, in the end, we were comfortable winners. That earned us the anticipated place in the quarter-finals and we said goodbye to Sydney's Concord Oval where we had played all our games; Australians have not much affection for the ground, which was developed by the New South Wales RFU as their headquarters in 1986, but as far as I was concerned it was fine. The weather was on our side, though, because it was warm and dry. It was a marked change from Twickenham, of course – a ground that could hold 20,000 as opposed to 60,000.

Not that 20,000 Aussies made their way out to the suburbs for the games but if the tournament from the outside appeared fairly low-key, we felt involved as players; our preparations were on a daily basis and we spent a lot of time watching televised games from New Zealand where the other three pools were played. There was some good rugby too: France and Scotland played a very good game and later France and Fiji produced an excellent quarter-final. However, second place behind Australia in our group meant that our quarter-final would be in Brisbane against Wales which, after what had happened earlier in the year, was not what we had hoped for. The Welsh had come through from the group including Ireland who, we had hoped, would be our opponents, but they were scheduled to meet Australia in Sydney 24 hours before our game with Wales.

There was a lot of press speculation about another possible confrontation but the Welsh had problems enough with injuries; they had to draft in two youngsters who were playing in Canberra, David Young and Richard Webster, and Young went straight in to prop against us on a wet Monday afternoon at Ballymore. It's difficult to add anything new to a match which has gone down in history as one of the worst England displays of recent times – or possibly any other time. Nothing went well for us; the playing surface is poor there, it was wet and we lost our way completely. In a sense the whole tournament was typical of England in the mid 1980s: a brave display against opponents whom we were not expected to beat (Australia), competent set-piece games against opponents who were inferior (Japan and the USA) but when called upon to respond to opponents of a similar standard, who knew our game well, we couldn't come up with the answers.

We expected to dominate up front, particularly against an untried Welsh prop, but we didn't and we lost Paul Rendall injured at much the same time as Gareth Roberts scored the first Welsh try. Indeed, that was a contributory factor because England had to put seven men into a scrum on our line before Gareth Chilcott came on, and the ball squirted out on what was the undefended open side, for Roberts to score. Robert Jones beat Richard Harding in a race for the second try and the final straw was the sight of John Devereux, fist raised in triumph, as he intercepted a pass and ran in under the posts for the third. End of match (16–3), end of tournament, one of the most disappointing moments of my rugby career; that match goes alongside the 1989 defeat in Cardiff and the 1990 grand-slam match in Scotland in my personal list of memories not to be recalled. It was the pits.

That night we went to a disco and found the Welsh there too, which was less than wonderful in the circumstances. The next day, as our coach sped past the Mayfair Crest Hotel in central Brisbane and headed for the airport, we saw Wales climbing on board their own coach; they were going forward in the competition and we were going home. The fact that they went on to a 49–6 hammering by New Zealand in the semi-final was of only marginal consequence as far as I was concerned. The adventure was over and England had hardly scratched the surface. That flight to London seemed to go on for ever; some of the team drowned their sorrows, but I just tried to sleep. At least that way you can forget, for a while, what has just happened.

That's looking at the inaugural World Cup with blinkers on. There is no comparison between the first and the second tournaments and I think it's a matter for regret that the first was not staged in Britain. In 1987 everything was low-key – certainly for us in Australia it was and I don't think it really registered at home. As a world competition there can be no complaints that New Zealand won, and deserved to. There were some cracking games, particularly the semi-final between Australia and France, but inevitably your view is coloured by the success or failure of your own side. That year might have seen the beginning of the evolution of the 1991 England side, but, at the time, we as players didn't look at it in that light.

9

Cooke's new recipe

Although 1987 did not seem so to the players, it was really the beginning: the beginning of a new attitude, of a brand new way of regarding rugby football. Previous teams had appreciated that the first-class game was more than recreation but their enthusiasm and dedication were inevitably coloured, either sooner or later, by the degree of preparation they found when they reached international level. Perhaps those brought up in the 'self-help' atmosphere of Margaret Thatcher's Britain of the 1980s viewed matters differently and were more receptive to the changes introduced by Don Rutherford, the Rugby Football Union's technical director, and the specialist assistance he introduced to make England players more athletic.

Rutherford had been working for nearly 20 years to bring England up to the elevated plane occupied by New Zealanders, South Africans and, latterly, Australians. It had been a long, hard slog, rewarded only once when England, in 1980, won a grand slam with a team elements of which had existed for the previous six years but which various selection panels had failed to bring together. Now, however, the selection process was being refined by a small RFU working party; the concept of a team manager, two team coaches and two national selectors was advocated, which was the first step – the second was to find the men to fill those posts which, in an amateur game, was never going to be easy.

Mike Weston, an England centre and captain during the 1960s, was the first choice as team manager, having just returned from the World Cup where he had fulfilled that role after two years as the traditional chairman of selectors. However Weston, an estate agent in Durham, was not permitted by the RFU committee to have the team he wanted –Martin Green, the World Cup coach, and Tony Jorden, as selectors, and Roger Uttley and Alan Davies as coaches. Just five weeks after his appointment was announced Weston resigned on principle and was succeeded by Geoff Cooke, team manager of the Northern Division and, at that stage, perhaps the only man in the country who had that sort of experience at representative level.

Cooke, then 46, brought with him a tighter concept of the management team. He changed the North's structure, replacing a selection panel with a manager – himself – and coach – David Robinson, the former Gosforth flanker – with room for an assistant coach if required. The North won the divisional championship with a team including Mike Harrison, Will Carling, Rory Underwood, Rob Andrew, Wade Dooley and Peter Winterbottom. Cooke made no secret of his intentions. 'I want to get strong control on all aspects of the international squad, using their abilities on and off the field,' he said. 'I want to be responsible for the strategy and tactics of the England side. There is organisation, personal man-management and style of play involved.'

Cooke, a Cumbrian, had spent most of his working life in Yorkshire and had been both player and administrator within the county. When he was appointed national manager he was principal sports development officer for Leeds City Council, though he subsequently became chief executive of the British Institute of Sports Coaches. His concept of a smaller team was adopted and John Elliott, a former Nottingham hooker and England triallist, who had been a divisional selector, was appointed national selector; two months later Uttley, a former England and British Lions No 8/flanker/lock, was named as coach to the senior England side while Davies and Robinson were to coach England B.

Cooke's stated aim, in the short term, was a minimum of two home wins in the 1988 championship. In the long term, he said, 'My ambition is to win the grand slam and unless the players have that ambition too we are not going places. It may take us some time to get there.'

After the 1987 World Cup there was a natural break. I had optimistically asked for six weeks away from work, to cover the duration of the tournament, but in the event when I reported back in mid June I was told: 'Right, you can start again next Monday!' There was no sense of tiredness from the tournament, only of disappointment that we had emerged in such a poor light, so it was probably good to get immersed in my normal day-to-day activity as quickly as possible.

Others players may have felt weary after what was, in effect, an elongated season but it has never taken me long to get back into the domestic pattern. I had another focal point anyway: Wendy and I were due to be married in September and had a lot of planning to do. We had already bought a cottage even though I was still supposed to be occupying my officer's quarters (I spent rather more time off base than the RAF technically permits) and we were saving hard. After my carefree bachelor existence money suddenly became rather tight since there were so many things we needed to buy; my car had gone a couple of days before I went to the World Cup and when I returned I bought a somewhat more modest Astra, in keeping with my restricted resources.

Rugby, for the time being, went by the board even though this was the first season of league rugby in England. Not that our wedding day did not have a certain rugby 'presence'. Wendy had been to Leicester to see me play – the first time she came we beat London Welsh 69–4 and I scored four tries, while the second time was the traditional dour encounter with Nottingham when I did nothing at all – so she had met people like Dusty Hare and Les Cusworth before. They were among six or seven Leicester players in East Halton that day and I think it was Les who, during the reception, turned on the television to discover that Leicester had just lost – to London Welsh.

I had hoped that Ian Goslin would be my best man, since I had spent so much time accepting his hospitality, but his job at Brize Norton took him to the USA reasonably frequently and he was overseas on our wedding day. So I had Mickey Harrison on stand-by – he wasn't worried at being, as it were, replacement – and on the Friday night I rang him to get him down to talk about arrangements and reminded him to bring his speech. Marion, his wife, answered and when I enquired after a speech she nearly fell over laughing because it was quite clear that Mickey was not aware of his additional responsibilities. It may have been my fault that I had omitted to tell him that Ian would not be available but he came down early and Marion followed later – with his suit, which Mickey had forgotten.

But after the wedding at St Peter's Church, East Halton, he gave an excellent speech at the reception, in a marquee at the house of Wendy's sister, Sue. There followed a buffet and disco in the evening and we were all having such a good time there seemed no reason to hurry away from one of the few occasions in your life when you have all the people you value most around you. Eventually we left around 11.30 p.m. and were heading towards the Humber bridge when Wendy gently enquired whether I had any money; a quick search of the car revealed that, though I was equipped with credit card to pay for the hotel where we were to begin our honeymoon, we had only about 26p in loose change which was not going to get us across the bridge with its toll of £1.20. So we turned round, went back to the farm where Wendy's parents live, removed the key from its hiding place and raided the church funds before heading with more confidence for the bridge, the hotel on the other side and, in due course, ten days in Tenerife.

When we returned there was a certain amount of ground to catch up on and, sadly, a termination of my playing days with Yorkshire. League rugby with Leicester meant that I could not be available for the Saturdays of the county championship, though I was happy enough to play in the couple of midweek fixtures if they wanted me; but Yorkshire felt it better to stick with those who were available on a regular basis and I could not quarrel with their decision. In some ways it was a relief, in that it was a reduction of my commitments, but disappointing because I had enjoyed myself with the county.

I had given the matter a lot of thought and Leicester, being the excellent club that it is, would not have batted an eyelid if I had said I wished to play county rugby at weekends. I have always admired their attitude in this respect; they have never put pressure on players to turn out for them, which has not always been the case with all England's leading clubs, notably in the West Country, where long-standing loyalties became very strained at times. So, as for many others that season and thereafter, the rugby became focused with the club and the division and it was a great delight for all at Welford Road when Tigers won the inaugural league championship. They did so in a far from easy season, when Graham Willars, the coach, was taken ill and Peter Wheeler added substantially to the coaching arrangements. But we played some exciting rugby and concluded with a lap of honour after defeating Waterloo in the match which brought Leicester the title; I was glad we were able to bring off the decisive victory at home, too, because Leicester's faithful supporters deserved the chance to celebrate together. It is, by some distance, the best-supported club in the country and the fans do so much to create the marvellous atmosphere in which the players revel.

While Leicester, captained by Paul Dodge although Les Cusworth took over for much of the time when Dodgie was injured, showed the way in league terms, the North also played an adventurous brand of rugby. It was only with England that the attractive rugby ceased. With the passing of time I came to understand the inhibitions which surrounded the national team, but also, what might have been possible given the right organisation.

As far as the changes which were taking place in team-management terms were concerned, I knew little more than what I read in the papers because there was no early-season gathering of the national squad. I knew Geoff Cooke from my days with Yorkshire and the North but his appointment as England manager, after Mike Weston resigned, was a bold decision by the RFU; perhaps it was the only option they had anyway, given Geoff's successful role with the North. I was delighted, though, because all of us who played for Yorkshire and for the division had great respect for what he had done; as well as acting as either chairman of selectors or manager, Geoff had also coached the backs while Dave Robinson coached the forwards for the North.

Apart from the fact that I believe he is a good backs coach, Geoff's great strength was to make us all think more about our own roles. He would ask us questions about what we were trying to do in different parts of the field, where to attack, how best to attack, rather than telling us what to do. What he told us then he has put into practice with England since. It was new and interesting and all the better coming from a man who was patently sincere, approachable, easy to get on with. Success in the divisional championship enabled him to take a comforting number of northerners into the national squad too, which led to whispers about northern bias and the famous remark attributed to Mark Bailey, the Cambridge University, Wasps and England wing, that 'if you didn't wear a flat 'at and have pigeon shit on your shoulders, you won't play for England'.

Perhaps that was inevitable but then, the team he had inherited was not exactly glowing with distinction and Geoff was looking ahead to the 1991 World Cup. He was trying to build a new structure, but since he was starting from fairly close to the bottom, he had a free hand. One of his problems was to decide on his fly-half from any one of Peter Williams, Rob Andrew – both of whom had been involved in the World Cup – Stuart Barnes and Les Cusworth. As it happened the choice was reduced to three when Stuart received a bad facial injury playing for Bath; Simon Hodgkinson was named in the first training squad but the names out of the hat for the trial in January put Les into the senior side and Rob into the juniors.

It was not a good beginning. The entire senior midfield was disrupted, Simon Halliday and John Buckton withdrawing injured and Les unable to train. On the Saturday the weather was appalling and the B XV, prepared by Alan Davies, won 13–7. So the team picked to play the first international of the season, against France in Paris, was a bit of a mix-and-match: Jeff Probyn, Mickey Skinner and Will

Carling won their first caps alongside players such as Les, Nigel Melville – who had retired the previous year after a neck injury – and John Orwin who may have thought their international careers behind them. But when you think about it, that XV included nine of the players who, four years later, were still there helping England to win a second successive grand slam. In selection terms that's not a bad record and it's an indication of why we have developed the success we have.

Roger Uttley's presence as coach was a comfort, although obviously he had more to do with the forwards. But from the first he and Geoff emphasised their desire for continuity; it was not to be a case of 'one mistake and you're out'. They encouraged positive thoughts and they wanted us to go out and play in the way of which they believed us capable. They preferred us to give 110 per cent and, if that was the case, a couple of errors could be excused. For those of us accustomed to Geoff's way from the North it was an extension of his approach then; we discussed the way the game should be played, the tactical approach with a stress on the three Cs – 'cool, calm, collected'.

Some of the guys were sceptical about his approach but it soon dawned that much of what both Geoff and Roger were saying was common sense. We were not given much hope, though, in the build-up to Paris and Roger produced his first, and probably best, team talk on the Friday before the game – he spoke to each of us individually, about the good points to our game, and the stirring atmosphere he created had the desired effect. We went out and took the game to the French; if we had taken our early chances we would have won. Will made a mess of a two-on-one and Kevin Simms passed when he could have scored but that is what sometimes happens to a team trying to develop confidence; we had yet to reach the stage where we could make our own luck. A penalty for a collapsed scrum brought France back to 9–6 before Laurent Rodriguez scored the winning try. It was almost in slow motion that I watched Mickey Harrison trying to pick up a bouncing ball on an uncharacteristically rough playing surface, only for Rodriguez to barge him aside and take on the ball for the game's only try and a French victory by 10–9.

At the final whistle there was intense disappointment that we had come so close to a completely unexpected victory, but Geoff underlined what a fantastic achievement it had been to come so close to the World Cup finalists and carry the game to them so well that they had been unable to play in the manner they wished. In the four years I had been playing for England there had seldom been so much commitment and it may be that the players were still riding high on that when the next game, against Wales, was played, because the same XV could find no way of imposing themselves at Twickenham and the Welsh won 11–3. It was the end of the line for Mickey and Les, and for Kevin Simms as it happened, and in the month that followed some interesting manoeuvres took place.

The captaincy passed from Mickey to Nigel Melville, Rob returned at fly-half and Simon Halliday came into the centre. It was interesting to see that the backs were presumed to have been at fault, either in defence or in lacking thrust in attack, and one further adjustment took me from the left wing to the right so that Chris Oti, from Cambridge University, could be included for his first cap. I was away in Cyprus on detachment, when the team was announced, and while I was there the local rugby club asked me to go along and do some coaching. We were in the bar having a drink afterwards when someone came in and said: 'I see Chris Oti's in the side to play Scotland.' That came as something of a shock. My initial reaction was to imagine I had been dropped, because Chris is a left wing and Mickey was captain, but since no one offered condolences I was somewhat confused.

Not that there was anything I could do about it until I returned home later in the week and discovered for certain which of us was playing on which wing. There had been no discussion about moving from left to right, which was what upset me most because there is a tendency, once you have been in the side for a while, to come to regard your position as 'home' – No 11, that's me – and to take pride in it. Many people might think that being in the England XV should be enough for anyone, but after 20 or so caps you come to feel that you can express yourself best in one particular position, and when you move away from that position it leaves a feeling of uncertainty.

I respected Chris as a talented opponent but I was somewhat bewildered by it all so the night I returned home I rang Geoff Cooke. Basically I wanted to know why the move had been made while Geoff, judging by our conversation, had it all worked out and it hadn't occurred to him there might be a problem – if only temporarily. He explained that he felt I would fit naturally on to the right wing, that my speed and strength coming in from the blind side could be used profitably, and since they felt the next best wing was Chris, who lacked international experience, it was better to put him into the position where he was most comfortable, the left.

There was no argument with Geoff about the situation, although I told him I felt I was better suited to the left. I had played on the right a couple of times, notably for England under-23 against England Students seven years earlier, but I was determined not to make a fuss about it, although there had been one or two questions asked in the press. If anyone asked me I simply said I preferred the left but I was happy to play for England anywhere, which did not stop one or two 'disgruntled' stories being printed which made their way up to Scotland before the match and were trotted out on television by Andy Irvine, who suggested I was in the wrong to air such thoughts before Chris's first match. That hurt a bit since I had gone out of my way to play down the situation while answering questions honestly.

It was not difficult to adapt my style of play. I had spent a career turning up on both wings for Yorkshire and the North while at Leicester I was used to filling in, as blind-side wing, at full-back when Dusty had moved up to take kicks to touch. Many times I have joined the line from full-back at club level and, in this instance, Leicester moved me to the right wing to play against Northampton just so that I could relocate myself. I had no worries about lines of running and I shrugged off any criticism and concentrated on doing well on that side of the field.

The match itself turned out to be a damp squib as a spectacle – although I do remember one spectacular break by Nigel Melville from an interception which took him 40 metres down the grandstand side with the entire back division screaming up in support but too deep for him to see and he was tackled into touch. Otherwise the match was memorable only for the remarks of Derrick Grant, the Scottish coach, afterwards who suggested that England had killed everything. But all in all we were happy enough to win 9–6 and revive a degree of confidence. It followed two previous defeats in the championship and the last two visits England had made to Murrayfield had ended badly so we were happy to retain the Calcutta Cup that we had held since the Twickenham win of 1987.

Not that the cup itself came into the best hands. It made an unscheduled departure from the banquet that evening and John Jeffrey and Dean Richards were subsequently suspended for having caused damage by using it as a rugby ball. Few of us were aware of any unauthorised pursuits at the time; it was a good night which Will remembers chiefly because Mickey Skinner emptied a bowl of cream over his head and tried to persuade the barman to have his jacket dry-cleaned at an unearthly hour. The following morning several of us took an early flight back to London and we didn't appreciate what had happened until articles started appearing in the papers. All of us have been to parties where a few people get carried away; the unwritten rule in the officers' mess is that, if any damage is caused, however inadvertently, those responsible will make good the damage. In this case I think the punishments dished out were about right. JJ was suspended until the start of the next season, which did not cause him to miss any significant representative occasions, and Dean was banned from the Dublin Millennium international although sentence was not pronounced until after we had played Ireland.

In retrospect the Irish game at Twickenham was where people started opening their eyes to what England might go on to achieve. For half the match there was nothing in it and Ireland led 3–0 through a dropped goal. Then Nigel Melville went off; more accurately, he was carried off. He had broken his leg and dislocated his ankle in a tackle, the culmination of a desperately unlucky career during which he received three major injuries. That he has managed to come through them all and still play again for Otley is a tribute to him.

At the time I just felt so sorry for him because he was a good friend, a fellow Yorkshireman, and there he was, down and out again. Richard Harding came on to play scrum-half and John Orwin took over as captain but I wasn't too aware of that because, unusually for me, I became very emotional about it. I wasn't angry at the Irish but I felt the need to do something to make up for Nigel's absence; Ireland offered me the opportunity by starting the second half kicking off into touch and from the scrum back we ran right with Webbie joining in. I found myself in space; I beat Keith Crossan then cut back inside Michael Bradley who was covering before Brendan Mullin brought me down just short of the line with a brilliant tackle. But I was able to feed the ball back and the forwards came over the top for Gary Rees to get the try.

The crowd was in raptures and it turned out to be the catalyst for a remarkable second half. Everything went like clockwork and we ran in six tries; Geoff's understanding of what I might do on the right came true and I spent the game making holes in the Irish defence. The ball began to flow left towards Chris and he scored the first hat-trick by an England player since 1980, which was great for him but left me feeling a bit impatient on the other side of the field. In the week preceding the game there had been some comment, not all of it favourable, about my apparent inability to score. One paper put up a chart of the progress of the eight current wings in the home unions and I was at the bottom of the list: 22 matches, four tries, which was a bit disheartening.

My big moment came from a line-out when Webbie came sailing

through on to a long pass from Will; I was up very flat and took the ball one-handed behind me and set off for the line. Bradley was covering again but I bumped him off and had to decide how best to use up the gathering forces of Trevor Ringland and Keither Crossan before feeding back to Webbie. But Trevor drifted off and I decided to keep going for the posts and launched myself into a huge swallow dive. I got to my knees and raised my arms to the North Stand; the pure relief of scoring what was my first championship try at Twickenham was overwhelming. Shortly afterwards I was over again. Two tries in one game: what was going on?

I'm still not sure why the game unfolded in exactly that way – whether it was Nigel going off in the way he did, which affected everyone, whether it was my run which led directly to a try immediately afterwards and lifted everyone, or whether our time had come. Certainly John Orwin's time had come, because he took over as captain during the game and remained in that position for the Millennium game and on tour in Australia and Fiji that summer. It was not an appointment that turned out well, in a year when England were led by five different people – Harrison, Melville, Orwin, Harding and Carling. I knew JO from RAF days and he was always his own man, a dominant character, calling the shots as he saw them and everyone accepted that; but leading the RAF was a bit different from leading England when greater diplomacy is required, both in handling team members and with the various public duties which devolve upon the captain.

Ironically I moved back to the left wing after that. Chris was not available for the summer tour because of university examinations, and the team for the match against Ireland to celebrate 1000 years of Dublin's fair city was to be chosen from the touring party. John Bentley began his brief international career before going to rugby league and I managed to get another try in a somewhat less distinguished win at Lansdowne Road.

Still, three wins in succession put England in a good mood for Australia and what was my first 'proper' tour. The World Cup a year earlier had been strange in that we were there for nearly four weeks and played only four games, but now we had a schedule of nine games, including three internationals, in much the same time span. There was the additional pleasure for me of being invited to join a World party to play Australia as a celebration of their Bicentenary as a country, an occasion when I thought Wendy might be able to share some of my good fortune by coming along too.

I had thought that, when such matches are played, wives and girlfriends get taken care of too and I made gentle enquiries along those lines. The Australian authorities said there was no objection so I told Wendy she was due for a week's holiday in Australia, which she thought was wonderful; but with each subsequent contact about the arrangements for the game in Sydney I had the sinking feeling that all expenses were not going to be paid for two of us. Eventually, about a week before we were due to fly out, I had to ask direct, 'Are you paying for Wendy to come over?' which produced a stifled laugh at the other end. It was not a happy position to be in because we would have been hard pressed to stump up nearly £1000 for the air fare, but Wendy's parents very kindly chipped in so she was able to go. I had somewhat innocently assumed that, such was the occasion, all would have been well and I was probably at fault for not clearing it up well before the departure date, but it is something to which the host unions on these special occasions may wish to give some thought themselves.

However, we arrived together in Australia and Wendy stayed out in the suburbs of Sydney while I found myself back at Rushcutters Bay where England had been quartered for the World Cup. Company on the long flight included Clive Rowlands, who was to manage the British Lions in Australia the next year, and Clive Norling, who was refereeing the match. I took the opportunity to tell Clive Rowlands that, if I was under consideration, I would like to be regarded as a left wing! The World XV proved to be a mixed bunch with a strong New Zealand thread running through it from Brian Lochore, the manager, down. We trained every morning and in the afternoons I would join Wendy for shopping and sightseeing.

The game itself, won by Australia 42–38, was not as memorable as it sounds although my attitude may be a bit jaundiced since I had to come off injured near the end. I had just managed to get round Ian Williams, the Australian wing, for about the first time – we saw a lot more of each other during the England tour and the year after in what became something of a personal duel – when he managed to catch me and swing me round, and my studs caught and I turned my ankle. I limped off and strapped up the foot and then went out to watch the end of the game, and Wendy came to see how I was; I later discovered that the England party, who by that time had arrived at Mackay in northern Queensland, were watching the match on television. Some concern was expressed when I went off but subsequently the cameras caught me sitting on a step, swigging a soft drink with Wendy alongside, and apparently Gareth Chilcott muttered: 'Look at that, he's found a girl already. I hope Wendy's not watching this.' At that point someone told Gareth it *was* Wendy, with a slightly amended hairstyle!

The next day was a dawn departure for Brisbane to link up with England. Having wangled a lift with *The Times* and the *Daily Telegraph* hire car I found, when I got out of bed, that my ankle was in agony. At least it gave me an excuse to get the press to carry my bags for me for the rest of the day, until we made it, via Brisbane, to Mackay where the first call was for 'Smurf' – Kevin Murphy, the England physiotherapist for so many seasons, who got his magic fingers to work. The ankle had not received the best of treatment thus far, in and out of hotels, up and down aircraft steps, so bags of ice emerged to get the swelling down and my recovery rate of only ten days speaks volumes for Smurf's skill which has proved of such value to England players.

However, there was no question of playing in the first two tour games, against Queensland Country and Queensland itself, both won although not without difficulty against the senior state side. In Brisbane I was training again, running straight lines if not too much twisting and turning, and the ankle felt good enough to tell Geoff Cooke that I would be fit for selection against Queensland B out on the Darling Downs, in Toowoomba. It took me a while to get into the game, on a rock-hard surface, but I managed a try and it was a comfort to finish the game. I needed it to get confidence back, to be involved once more, and that was certainly the case since I played the next three games too.

The first of those three was, in fact, the first test which, you might say, got off to a runaway start. Nick Farr-Jones tried a long pass which Bryan Barley intercepted and gave me the ball with about 60 metres to go. I was outside Andrew Leeds, their full-back, and made it into the corner; later in the match I had another run but Ian Williams got back to haul me down which suggests, that summer at least, he was faster than me. We scored another long-range try, through John Bentley, and again through an interception after which he had to hold off James Grant on what must have been an 80-metre run to the posts, all of which helped to give us a 13–3 lead at which Michael Lynagh nibbled away with a series of penalties and Australia took a 22–16 win. Michael found his touches magnificently that day, gobbling up 60 or 70 metres at a time, and we had not the confidence in ourselves that we developed later.

The game against an invitation XV in Adelaide which followed was

notable for the absence of the visiting team when the anthems were
being played. It was a night game, with Rob captaining from centre,
and our exit from the changing room coincided with Nigel Redman's
absence in the toilet. When we were finally ready to trot out Geoff
stopped us in the tunnel because the national anthem was already
sounding around the stadium; that meant a heavy punishment for
Nigel at the next players' court. He was ordered to stand in front of the
presiding judge, Paul Rendall, and sing the national anthem – and he
dried up after the first couple of lines!

At that stage of the tour we were still reasonably happy; we had lost
the first test but were building ourselves up for the second, still hoping
to become the first English side to win an international in Australia.
That hope receded at the Concord Oval where we played New South
Wales; it had been a wet Australian winter and the playing surface was
saturated, yet they still insisted on playing curtain-raisers before the
main game, which I could not understand then and still don't.

Amid the mud Brian Smith, at fly-half for NSW, played very well,
kicked his goals and they emerged with a 23–12 win. England played
poorly, staying in touch only through Jonathan Webb's penalties, and
it was there that rifts started to appear in the touring party, an 'us and
them' division between backs and forwards. The backs had not played
well but against New South Wales the forward effort died and some
serious questions began to be asked about John Orwin's leadership.
To make matters worse, some players were disgruntled to find press
reports filtering back from England about players' court proceedings,
which are only light relief for the tour party and which seem to me to
play no part in serious reporting of a rugby tour. There had already
been some reports that players were critical of the boots they were
given to wear, as part of an RFU deal with Nike, the sportswear firm,
which had raised the hackles of the management and further adverse
comment we could have done without.

It's worth saying how much court sessions conducted in the right
way, can help a tour. England teams have been noted particularly for
their courts, in which different players have specific 'legal' functions
and hand out humorous sentences for alleged misdemeanours. If the
punishments become vindictive, then it helps no one, and there might
have been an element of that early in the tour; but when times are
difficult, as they were in Argentina in 1990 for example, then the court
sessions are a way of letting off steam, of raising morale, of cheering
players up.

Some of the fundamental disagreement in Australia centred around the tactical approach, at least as far as I was concerned. With Richard 'Corkie' Harding at scrum-half there was bound to be a lot of chasing of kicks, and I admit I'm not one of the world's best when it comes to that. I found myself chasing kicks all day, and at that time we did not have a proper appreciation of the ten-metre offside law which the Australians had perfected; so I would set off in pursuit of a long kick, then go into reverse when Michael Lynagh or David Campese sent it back over my head. Now we spread players in layers across the field, either as support for our catcher or to pressurise the opponents' receiver, but in 1988 we had not worked out our response and I received a lot of flak from Corkie about not being in position to chase when he put up yet another box kick.

In my own mind I was still getting back into the game myself, after my ankle injury, and we had not put as much thought into our own positions on the field as we came to do over the next four years. I made the point, when we met as a team to discuss the NSW defeat, that the kicks needed to be shorter because as it was the Australians were returning them with interest and I was effectively out of the game. Neither Corkie nor David Robinson, the assistant coach, were very impressed; they told me I should run faster to get back onside and seemed to feel I had something of an 'attitude' problem. So I wasn't very happy when we set off for Wollongong, to the south of Sydney, for the midweek game with New South Wales B. Barry Evans, who played on the other wing with me at Leicester and was about to win his first cap, joined me for a long walk down the beach at Wollongong and gave me the chance to get everything, including, I dare say, more than a touch of home-sickness, off my chest.

Barry and Andy Robinson both made their international debuts in the second meeting with Australia, a game which was prefaced by one of the more embarrassing team talks from John Orwin. Sadly JO had lost a lot of respect during the tour; he wasn't fit and where he intended a stirring rallying call to the troops, he failed miserably. David Robinson, too, failed to hit the right note as far as I was concerned, harking back to what I had said after the NSW game and telling me, with a great swat over the head which was meant to be encouraging but wasn't, that forwards did all day long what I had complained about.

We started the game well enough and I squeezed into the corner for the first of the tries which have become a bit of a trademark, the one-handed touchdown at the flag. But we ended a well-beaten side at 28–8; everything the Australians tried came off – as it did when they beat us on tour in 1991 – and Campo carved us up. We thought we might exploit Glen Ella's return to the centre but he had the last laugh with one of their four tries.

Although we had still a match in Fiji to go it was the end of so many hopes, and of JO as an international player. Having known him from RAF teams for so many years I should have recognised that he was not the sort of person who should have been put in charge of a national touring side; perhaps, in his own eyes, he had reached the top and that was enough. He seemed to expect that others would defer to him, as captain, in whatever circumstances: Simon Robson, the Moseley scrum-half, worked a move from a line-out incorrectly in training and JO smacked him hard across the face for it. On another occasion a couple of us were waiting for physiotherapy when John came in and demanded a rub-down before he went to the pub, only to be told by Smurf in no uncertain terms that others were waiting and so could he.

Our mood was not improved by the Australians not swapping shirts in the traditional manner; players look forward to collecting these 'souvenirs' of matches but the Aussies never seem to have been keen on the idea and we were left with a job lot of jerseys, some of which had clearly never emerged on an international field. So we flew out to Fiji feeling very morose, most players considerably hung over after drowning their sorrows the night before. On these occasions I am usually appointed duty boy because I don't drink but it was hard work getting everyone on the coach in time, even harder when no trace could be found of John Bentley. Geoff Cooke and I searched through every room we had occupied at the Camperdown Travelodge but there was no sign until we asked a maid to unlock one of the spare rooms and there was 'Bentos' flat out under the sheets with a mate from Headingley, having 'celebrated' not wisely but too well. Geoff and I burst out laughing and promptly sent for a camera to record the happy scene before dragging Bentos from his slumbers and piling him on to the coach.

When we arrived in Fiji JO closed what was becoming an increasingly unhappy chapter. We trained in Suva on the day we arrived, in exceptionally humid weather, and halfway through the session John suddenly stopped, walked off and told the management he wasn't fit. You could tell that he didn't like the heat and didn't fancy the game. He was pulled out of the side to play Fiji, with an ankle injury, and Nigel Redman came into the second row with Corkie taking over for his one match – and his last international – as England captain.

We all knew that this was not calculated to produce an expansive game. On the Wednesday night – the international was played on a Thursday – Corkie came out with his famous team talk, running through the various situations which might arise. Whatever the question, the answer was a kick from the base of the scrum, from the ruck, from the line-out! This was the match which earned Rob Andrew a cap at full-back; we had all expected Ray Adamson, the Wakefield player, to win his first cap because Webbie had to go home after Australia, but though Ray had enjoyed a brilliant season with Yorkshire and the North at home, he totally lost his confidence on tour and was never able to make the final step up. It was a great shame.

We won 25–12 which was something of a consolation at the end of the tour; I picked up a couple of tries, Gary Rees collected a fist in the face from Mosese Taga, the Fijian prop, who was sent off, and David Egerton collected the shortest cap in history by replacing Gary deep in injury time. 'Have I got time to do my boots up?' he said. 'No, get on the pitch,' we all screamed at him and he trotted on, watched Stuart Barnes take a kick to touch, and the whistle went. At least we were able to have a genuine celebration with the Fijians before the long, long trip home.

At the end of it all it may have seemed that England had taken no substantial steps forward but I think in his mind Geoff Cooke knew far better what had to be done and began to set out his stall as to how he could achieve it. That was his first opportunity to get a squad together over a long period and assess the situation and how far he had to go. He seemed to get on well enough with Alan Davies and David Robinson, as a team, although the following year Alan and Robbo were replaced as B-team coaches and Alan subsequently went on to coach Wales. I think Alan, at that time, was a couple of steps ahead of a lot of the players, particularly the forwards; as a squad we needed to keep things simple so as to establish confidence, some kind of pattern, and the forwards didn't take to him.

And at the back of many people's minds was the thought that the Australians were due to visit us in the autumn and perhaps we could show them that we had something better to offer. We did.

10

The year of the Lion

It had become painfully apparent during the 1980s that the playing standards of the southern-hemisphere countries had advanced while the successes of the British Isles in 1971 and 1974, and the golden era of Welsh rugby, were becoming a distant memory. The 1983 British Lions in New Zealand had been whitewashed 4–0 in the international series; England had been beaten on tour in South Africa (1984) and New Zealand (1985) and the dominant team in the 1987 World Cup was New Zealand, only France upholding northern-hemisphere pride with a remarkable semi-final victory over Australia.

England's failure in Australia in 1988 coincided with the visit by Wales – winners of the triple crown that year – to New Zealand, during which they suffered defeat in both internationals by 52–3 and 54–9. At last it was brought home to administrators in Britain that though the Five Nations championship was a remarkable crowd-pulling tournament, the standard was quite frequently mediocre. Scotland may have recognised this earlier than others and their answer was to institute a series of tours, taking either their senior squad or a development squad overseas most years so that they could extract the most from their limited playing resources.

England's problem had always been the number of players available, many of them playing rugby of a dubious quality, and lack of consistency in selection. But a harder edge was developing because of the introduction of league rugby; Rory's club, Leicester, won the inaugural Courage Clubs Championship in 1988 and one of the effects of competitive rugby was to draw together leading players in a handful of first-division clubs. Bath dominated the English cup competition during the 1980s and, late in the decade, Harlequins came to challenge them. At the same time, in a contracting job market, many players moved from the provinces, particularly from the north of England, to London and the consequence was the capital's domination of the divisional championship.

The rise of league rugby coincided with the drive towards improved fitness which the Rugby Football Union's technical officers preached, and the feeling among many players that it was about time some pride was restored to British rugby. A British Lions tour to Australia was scheduled for the summer of 1989 which offered an alluring prospect for those who believed the southern hemisphere had had their own way for too long.

Another season, another tour. Those England players who had expressed on the flight home from Australia in June their anxiety for another crack at the Wallabies were going to get it because the increasingly busy schedule of tours brought them to England and Scotland for the first time since their grand-slam tour of 1984 and they were matched against all four divisional sides, England B and the Combined Students before the international with England at Twickenham.

But there was more to it than that, because it was obvious that a new team captain would have to be appointed – we had gone through four that year, Mickey Harrison, Nigel Melville, John Orwin and Richard Harding, the last two forming something of a stopgap if only on grounds of age. We had not speculated much on the likely candidates because the squad had not been together since dispersing from Heathrow, but there were not too many in the queue for the job. In terms of pure international experience I had more caps than anyone else – Peter Winterbottom didn't start that season because he had spent the summer playing in South Africa and returned home with an injury – and not far behind were Wade Dooley and Rob Andrew.

But the first task as far as most of us were concerned was to take on the Wallabies for our respective divisions. London fired the opening shot with a 21–10 win which ran them ragged and the North followed suit, though not in such an impressive manner, on a damp Wednesday afternoon at Otley where we won 15–9. Most of us had played together a month or so earlier in a charity game at Gateshead when we laid eyes for the first time on Dewi Morris, a scrum-half who had emerged from Winnington Park to join Liverpool St Helens and linked up with Peter Buckton to great effect. We thought even more of him when Dewi finished off a 60-metre move to score the try that gave the North their victory over the Australians, the first time I had ever been in a side that had beaten them. It was sweet, too, for Wade, Rob, John Buckton and Will Carling, all of whom had been on the wrong end of the results in Australia during the summer.

All of a sudden the Australians began to look far more vulnerable. They were without Michael Lynagh at that early stage though they sent for him because of injury problems in midfield, and many of them had not played rugby for some weeks. Though they beat England B quite comfortably they went down again to the South-west division and there was an air of expectancy growing. None the less it was only a week before the international that the selectors came up with a reshaped England side that included first caps for Dewi, Andy Harriman and Paul Ackford. We had all been so busy on divisional business that there had been no national squad meetings before then and, frankly, Paul's name meant very little to me at the time.

The captaincy, of course, went to Will. The meeting we had that weekend remains clear in my mind. Geoff Cooke, in his preliminary remarks to the squad, said that in picking the captain the selectors had gone for someone who would be a fixture in the side and would still be there in 1991 for the World Cup. My own mental list of possible captains did not put Will near the top, purely on the basis of seniority; Dean Richards was one possibly, Brian Moore another. It came as a surprise to me and, judging by the gasps that went round the room, to others too. It was not an easy moment for Will either, and he looked a bit uncomfortable, but Geoff explained his belief that Will had the right credentials for the job.

It was a bold choice, very forward-looking, but one that I could accept. I did not put myself anywhere near the captaincy anyway but possibly the lack of outstanding candidates at that time made the long-term decision easier to make. Will, who had heard the decision himself only a few days earlier, didn't say much to us as a squad at the time and most of us went away to digest what we had been told. Will had then, and still has, a very mature head on young shoulders, to which his military background and psychology studies at Durham University have contributed. What he had still to do was earn the respect, as a player, of the senior members of the squad, particularly the forwards, and he went a long way to doing so in his first game as captain – the 28–19 victory over Australia.

For all of us it was pay-back time, after the failures of the summer tour. Will gave a sense of direction even though he had been in the national side for less than a year; he was someone it was easy to follow. As a player he possesses a beautiful pass and he has the strength to break tackles and great pace – not bad attributes for a centre. When he first arrived on the representative scene with the North he fitted in very well; he didn't try to impose himself and, in his words, he was just pleased to be playing alongside people like Rob Andrew and Rory Underwood.

The match itself was partly the result of what the divisions had already achieved, partly a lack of confidence among the Australians compared with the summer and partly the new spirit in the England squad. The backs had been reshaped and encouraged to play an expansive game, and although we went 9–3 down in the early stages, Dewi scored a try when Campo tried running out of defence and was caught, with Andy Robinson charging down a kick. We even came back from the disappointment of conceding an interception try to Campo, for which I blame myself: I was over on the right-hand side of the field and by trying to take my marker out, delayed the pass to Jonathan Webb. He tried to take-and-give all in one movement and Campo found the ball in his hands as he went for the smother tackle.

So I had something to make up for when Robbo took a long throw over the top of a line-out and found Simon Halliday. Hallers went through a couple of tackles, popped the ball to Will and though we had a ruck there, Paul Ackford bobbled a pass out to Rob who got his pass to me away behind two Australians and I squeezed into the north-west corner with a one-handed touchdown. My second try came when Rob collected a drop-out and Dean went storming through in a rare 20-metre dash, people dropping off him, before feeding David Egerton (a flanker that day) and Robbo who gave me a lovely pass and room to get outside the cover and over in the same corner.

But even when we went to 22–13 the Australians were not done. James Grant came back with a try and it was only when we were able to take advantage of their losing possession that Will's break led to Hallers scoring a long-distance try. It's difficult to describe how pleased and relieved we were, and how much enjoyment we derived from the support – it was a long time since a Twickenham crowd had enjoyed such a feast. In the light of subsequent events – the Australians went on to beat Scotland 32–13 – we felt even better about it and although I was on the losing end in their last two matches (against the Combined Services and the Barbarians), it left England in a reasonably optimistic frame of mind for the Five Nations championship, which was to start against Scotland at Twickenham. Even better, a month later I received confirmation of my promotion to Flight Lieutenant.

However, the championship opened indifferently. The Scots denied us a lot of the ball and Webbie, who had had a cartilage operation over the Christmas period, missed a few kicks; to make matters worse, we were guilty of not clearing up dropped possession properly and when

Webbie dropped a high ball, Chris Oti and I stood around looking at it while John Jeffrey barged through and beat us to the touchdown. Chris's return meant that I switched back to the right wing that season but that incident, which helped Scotland to a 12–12 draw, fuelled the criticism of the three of us – Chris, Jonathan and me – as a defensive trio. It had happened before but this time the response was more constructive; Geoff talked to us all about it and we worked in training about the exact positions each of us should assume, what the nearest wing should do to help the full-back, while the second wing should take up a role 15 metres back watching for spilled ball. There was a lot more structure to it which had not happened before, and over the years the back-three defence has improved significantly.

Indeed before the next match, against Ireland, the squad asked for extra training – penance for the draw? At least it worked because we played a tighter game at Lansdowne Road which, in retrospect, could be seen as a preview of the way the British Lions were to play in Australia that summer. England had brought back Mike Teague at blind-side flanker to play alongside Dean, and the style of play which had beaten Australia receded into the distance in a 16–3 win which brought tries for Dean and what amounted to a 'shared' score for Dewi and Brian Moore who went over together.

Forward play dominated the match with France, too, which makes it ironic that Will should have been acclaimed for the try that he scored, his first in international rugby! It was the result of a move which went wrong, though we have since brought it into our repertoire – with modifications. What should have happened was Chris Oti coming off his wing to switch with Will but he came slightly too early and when Will went to make the pass Chris was virtually standing still beside him; but he had confused the French cover and Will decided to keep going and the way to the line opened in front of him. It was a dream start and a dream finish, when Robbo scored the second try in an 11–0 win. I had not been on the winning side against France before and suddenly there was a prospect of winning the championship that season.

The prospect died on a miserable March afternoon in Cardiff. There had been no lack of people telling us that if we could not beat Wales in Cardiff that day we never would, because the Welsh had lost all their matches that season. The build-up in the papers was as intense as ever; we were out-and-out favourites to break the Cardiff hoodoo which had survived since 1963 and Wales, at home, were written off. When we ran out at the Arms Park there was a nasty breeze and the rain was pouring down, and Robert Jones, the Welsh scrum-half, had one of his best tactical games, notably in the second half.

We lost Teaguie right at the start, in a collision from the kick-off. It affected us in two ways – psychologically it was a blow to lose a player with the match hardly begun and also much of our driving forward play that season had been constructed around Mike and Dean. He was replaced by Gary Rees, who is a good flanker but different to Mike in how he plays the game. None the less we established a 3–0 lead, then a 9–6 lead with Rob and Paul Thorburn, the Welsh captain, swapping kicks. Then came the period immediately after half-time, in which England have regularly let themselves down, though on this occasion it became a personal nightmare.

We had kicked off long and Thorburn, rather than finding touch, kicked to the open side where I was and I knocked on. Wales had a scrum on halfway and up came a high ball from Paul Turner to my wing and just outside the 22. I caught it with plenty of time and was about to pass back to Webbie when Gary Rees appeared in between us, running back in support; I checked and tried to lob over Gary a pass which Webbie could not take. The ball was hacked on and Kerry Fitzgerald, the Australian referee, gave the try to Mike Hall. The conversion made it 12–9 and thereafter Wales would not let us away from the corridor down our left: Robert Jones chipped into the space, forcing Chris and Webbie to cling to the touchline, and Robert Norster had a marvellous afternoon at the line-out.

At the time, disappointed though I was to have made the error which gave Wales their try, England were not out of contention because there was plenty of time to go. But the way Wales played induced an increasing sense of desperation. I tried not to dwell on the mistake but when the final whistle sounded it was horrid, one of the few occasions when I felt I was completely to blame for defeat. Some of the lads had tried to console me in the dressing room afterwards but I was in tears; I sat on the bench, head in hands. I have never watched the video of that match although I have seen my mistake again – in a 'horror movie' which Geoff had made for us the following year, a review of the worst moments during England matches under his management. We have watched that particular video before each Welsh match since 1989, just a a reminder of what can go wrong.

At the end of the day you have to realise that such moments can occur in any sport and learn to come to terms with them. There is nothing you can do to bring the moment back but it is not so much a matter of forgetting it ever happened as one of increasing your determination not to let it happen again. Defeat was not improved by the knowledge that we had let slip the championship to France, who beat Scotland that same day, and our minds were more on that subject than the speech Thorburn made at the banquet that evening which began with a request that Steve Jones, the correspondent of the *Sunday Times*, should leave the room because the Welsh captain considered him 'the scum of the earth'. It came as a complete shock to us and the only sound was of chins hitting the floor in amazement! Not many of us were aware of the reason why Paul began his speech that way; Steve Jones had expressed the view in an article that week that it might be beneficial to Welsh rugby if Wales lost. Some of the England players may have admired Paul for having the courage to say what many of us sometimes think, but there were better ways of going about it and I think Paul realised that later. You can tell a journalist that you think what he has written is rubbish – which gives him the chance to come back too – and that is what Paul should have done, though I believe that he and Steve made their peace later.

For us, though, that was a side issue. Reviewing the season England could only be disappointed that we had done so well against Australia yet reverted to a forward-dominated style for the Five Nations. We were still trying to identify the style of play that suited us best: we floundered against the Scots, we played in wet conditions in Ireland, while against France it was force against force, two very big packs and a good set of backs against us. Even though we had registered five points in the championship, which had not happened for seven years, we could not but regret a missed opportunity and, personally, a disappointing season.

The consolation came a week later: selection for the Lions tour to Australia in the summer, one of ten Englishmen in the party of 30. That came as a huge relief after a championship during which I had scored no tries and had been involved in a couple of expensive mistakes. Both Chris Oti and I were chosen as wings, along with Ieuan Evans and Mike Hall – normally a centre – of Wales. Everyone had been aware of the tour but first thoughts had always been on the championship; having said that, it was a thrill to be part of the first Lions tour since 1983. Only two players in 1989, Robert Norster and Donal Lenihan, had gone to New Zealand six years before and although some of us had played in the 1986 celebration game at Cardiff, that was hardly the same as a fully fledged tour, so it was a totally new experience.

It was one more of my ambitions realised. Even though I have now played in grand-slam winning sides and appeared in a World Cup final, a Lions tour remains a highlight and can do so much for Five Nations rugby – by bringing together players from the four home unions and establishing friendships which can contribute to a more generous approach when we meet in our national teams. Maybe it's worth reminding people that the 1987 fracas when Wales and England met in Cardiff occurred four years after the last Lions tour. When you are together for two months you can't help but get to know other people better, understand what makes them tick and why they play rugby the way they do.

England had one more match before the Lions came together, in Romania, and Leicester had a cup final to contest. It was the first time I had played in the cup final (I joined the club the season after their previous appearance, in 1983) and it proved a marvellous occasion. A knee injury had kept me out of the quarter-final victory over Wasps but Leicester had beaten Harlequins, the holders, in the semi-final and Dusty Hare and Les Cusworth demonstrated to all and sundry that they still knew more than most about how to win a game of rugby. The final at Twickenham, against Bath, was Dusty's last match before he retired and we would have loved to win and send him off in a blaze of glory, but it was not to be. We really carried the game to Bath in the first half but the supply of ball dried up after the interval and Stuart Barnes darted over for the winning try just before the final whistle, Leicester losing 10–6.

At much the same time, England lost Will Carling, as did the Lions. A shin condition forced him to surrender his place for the match in Bucharest and up stepped a young man called Jeremy Guscott – who also took Will's place as a Lion. It was quite an experience to visit Romania before the revolution and not one that many of us wanted to repeat in a hurry. We had been warned about the possibility of people listening to conversations and advised not to say anything critical of the Ceausescu regime, which then had only seven months to run; but we didn't notice secret police everywhere, rather the misery on the faces of the local population, the grey and hopeless looks of people queuing for what little was on sale in the shops.

The match itself was every bit as one-sided as 58–3 suggests, though if you suggested that 14 Englishman heaped misery upon them while one of them – me – did not, you would not be so far wrong. The good times were on hand particularly for Chris, with four tries, and Jerry, with three, and Simon Hodgkinson who kicked 19 points on his debut. It was Jerry's good fortune to be playing in the centre with Simon

Halliday, his clubmate from Bath, and he took full advantage, dummying his way through for two of his three scores; I remember them because I was the one he dummied!

The Lions assembled at the end of May in London, a party which, initially, was very Scottish in outlook. That was hardly surprising since the coach, Ian McGeechan, and the captain, Finlay Calder, were both Scots. Finlay and his colleagues from the Scotland back row, John Jeffrey and Derek White, were dab hands at organising and when we first came together for fitness testing Finlay had expressed some dismay about the levels of fitness of the other players compared with the Scots. In fact the English players, having had the international in Romania to prepare for, were pretty fit but there were at that stage some elements of national rivalries.

That's the way it is – you stick to your own groups. It's happened at times with players from the same club within a national squad but basically you had two big groups within the Lions party, from England and Scotland, who were perhaps a bit wary of each other – particularly after the two dog fights we had made of the last two Calcutta Cup matches. The Welsh were a bit disgruntled at their recent fall from grace and the Irish, a great set of lads, were just happy to be on tour. But during the first fortnight of the tour we became less and less a bunch of English, Scots, Irish and Welsh and more the British Lions. It took a couple of games for us really to come together but Perth was a good place to start, because of the climate and the hard game that Western Australia gave us. You don't expect to come off the pitch and hear the opposition saying 'Give those Aussies stick', but since Western Australia included 13 ex-patriot New Zealanders, we shouldn't have been surprised!

Perth was brilliant and I don't think I've ever stayed in such a good hotel as the Burswood; happily I was not among those to lose money in the casino complex attached to the hotel. We were able to work together as a team well away from the centres of media and public interest, Sydney and Brisbane, and on our way east we had another hard game against Australia B in Melbourne. So by the time we arrived in Brisbane to play Queensland, the leading state side, we had quite a lot of work under our belts; there we met Rob Andrew who had flown out as a replacement for Paul Dean, the Irish fly-half who damaged his knee so badly in the first game that he returned home and, in fact, did not play international rugby again.

We were a proper touring party by then; there were times when people went off into little groups and got things off their chests to friends but generally the atmosphere was good. I was given charge of the rooming list by Finlay, on the basis that a back and a forward of different nationalities roomed together so as to help people forget for a while their nationalities. The problem was that no one wanted to share with either Teaguie or Scott Hastings, both of whom snore very loudly! My answer was to put them both together but Mike objected to Scott so they both wound up with separate rooms.

Rob received his first game at the tourist centre of Cairns, against Queensland B where our off-the-field activities made more headlines than the game. One of the local attractions is wild-water rafting in inflatable rafts down the Barron River and several Lions decided this was just the job for an afternoon off; my raft included Roger Uttley, Teaguie and Dai Young – at least, it did before we capsized halfway down the course. We were all thrown into the river and I surfaced under the raft itself and could see nothing. I ducked down and came up on the other side to hear our guide shouting, 'Keep to the left'. The right-hand side of the river included a dangerous cluster of rocks and though three of us emerged safely enough, Dai Young was hanging on desperately to avoid being swept into these rocks. Fortunately he managed to extract himself and we carried on down, but looking back I don't think I want to repeat the exercise. The tabloids back home loved it, though I don't think that's the reason why Dai subsequently went over to rugby league. I got wet again at Cairns but this time back at the Hilton Hotel where the boys decided to celebrate my 26th birthday by throwing me into the swimming pool dressed in my tour No 1s.

During the first month expectations grew. Having overcome the Queensland hurdle in a very hard game – there were accusations in the Australian press of intimidation by the Lions after that match – the Lions approached the first test with an unbeaten record. But even though we had been on tour for a month we had not really gelled and the XV selected for the international, which was influenced by injury to players like Mike Teague and Scott Hastings, had not played together. We were in for a real shocker at the Sydney Football Stadium. Everything clicked for Australia on the day; they ran in four tries to none, and as a team we weren't good enough to stop them. We lost 30–12 and, with only a week before the second test, suddenly the success or failure of the entire tour was in the balance; up to that point it had gone reasonably well but the margin of defeat turned everything upside down. We arrived for the midweek game against Australian Capital Territory in Queanbeyan a very introspective party knowing

ABOVE: *The team that paved the way for the renaissance of English rugby – John Elliott, Geoff Cooke and Roger Uttley*

MIDDLE: *Patrice Lagisquet – my most respected and difficult opponent*

BELOW: *January 1990, Ireland at Twickenham and I have just scored the try that made me England's record-holder of tries with 19*

LEFT: *Yippee!! A sudden release of emotion as the final whistle goes and we have won the grand slam*

BELOW: *Twickenham's West Stand as it has seldom been seen – England celebrate the 1991 grand slam outside the changing room. Note who is holding the lemonade bottle!*

OPPOSITE ABOVE: *One Wallaby that didn't get away in July 1991 – Marty Roebuck on the receiving end of one of my tackles. It didn't help us much – we lost 40–15*

OPPOSITE BELOW: *World Cup 1991 – Italy's Troiani gets in a tackle but can't stop me scoring England's first try that day*

The 1991 World Cup squad. Back row, left to right: S. Hodgkinson, D. Morris, J. Guscott, M. Teague, P. Winterbottom, N. Heslop, J. Leonard, B. Moore; middle row: S. Halliday, J. Webb, D. Richards, P. Ackford, M. Skinner, W. Dooley, N. Redman, G. Pearce, J. Probyn, C. Oti; front row: D. Pears, R. Underwood, R. Hill, W. Carling, R. Andrew, P. Rendall, G. Rees, J. Olver

The 1992 grand slam squad. Standing, left to right: R. Hill, N. Heslop, T. Rodber, J. Webb, D. Richards, M. Bayfield, W. Dooley, M. Skinner, P. Winterbottom, J. Probyn, J. Leonard, M. Hynes. Seated: R. Underwood, J. Guscott, R. Andrew, W. Carling, B. Moore, D. Morris, S. Halliday, D. Pears, J. Olver

LEFT: *A proud moment as I lead out England against Scotland at Murrayfield on 26 October 1991, the occasion of my 50th cap*

MIDDLE: *Evading Craig Chalmers' tackle. I eventually score a try at all the major grounds I have played in – this one at Murrayfield in January 1992*

BELOW: *Now is the time to say goodbye – the second grand slam has been won after the defeat of Wales in 1992 and for me it's the end of the road*

Ieuan Evans denies me the try that would have given me the full set for the season. England v Wales, Twickenham 1992

The four of us together – me, Wendy, Rebecca (left) and Alexandra

that we were at crunch point; defeat, we felt, would really put the tour on the rocks.

Finlay, I know, was desperately disappointed after the first test and the effect of the defeat, and the criticism we endured really drew us together – it was the Lions against the rest of the world. For a time against the ACT it looked as though the rest of the world was winning because they went ten points up by half-time. In the stand the tour management looked grim but we came back in the second half to win 41–25, with Peter Dods kicking 21 points, and for the first time it looked as though Scott and Jerry would become the centre pairing for the test. The selection meeting for the second test must have been worth listening to because five changes were made, four of them involving Englishmen. Jerry and Rob came into the backs, Wade Dooley and Teaguie into the pack which included five England forwards.

It was a brave decision to drop Robert Norster, given the supremacy he had enjoyed over Wade at home, but he had not played well on tour while the balance of the back row for the first test had left something to be desired. There was a stunned silence when the team was read out and the Welsh contingent was amazed to find Robert was out. But we all knew that this was a do-or-die test; we had read the papers, we had seen what Australia thought of us – which didn't amount to much – and there seemed even to have been some criticism, which I found hard to believe, from Will Carling back home, who had been doing some commentary work for the BBC. When we saw a transcript of what Will had said we realised that some of his remarks, which appeared in a British paper, had been taken out of context, but nothing could change the significance of the game at Brisbane's Ballymore ground.

There was a lot of tension in the dressing room. This was one of the biggest games I have ever played in – I would compare it with the grand slam games of 1990 and 1991 with the difference that in 1990 England were expected to win whereas against France the following year there was no such favouritism. And in Australia we were on our own and no one expected us to win. We went out and played tremendously well; we had several scoring chances which we couldn't take but we hung in there and the forwards were outstanding. We went out there intending to hassle the Australian backs as much as possible, and the most effective way of doing that was at source – at scrum-half. It was a quite deliberate policy for Robert Jones to snap away at Nick Farr-Jones like a terrier, giving him no space at all, getting in his way, putting him off his game. Maybe because of the tension of the game Robert became carried away and the two of them had a go at each other at one stage. The other main incident for which that game is remembered is when David Young, the Welsh prop, stamped on Steve Cutler, Australia's lock, which I didn't see because I was on the far side of the field. I think if he had done it at home he would have been sent off, simple as that, but René Hourquet, the French referee, did not do so. There was a huge uproar about it, replays on television and demands that Dai should be sent home. He was in the wrong and he was reprimanded by Clive Rowlands, the tour manager, but we were as much annoyed by the attitude of the Australian press which seemed to paint their own players whiter than white. Because of that incident we were labelled thugs but Mike Hall had suffered just as badly when the Lions played Queensland.

The Australians may have been caught on the hop by the ease of their first-test win. We had to improve on that showing and we did, in all areas but notably at fly-half where Rob came in and played the first of a series of greatly matured games which have been so crucial in England's subsequent success. Even so we were three points down going into the final quarter and the clock had only four minutes left when Teaguie drove in midfield, Robert Jones broke to the left and I scissored with him before giving the ball inside; we rucked and Scott sent out a Barnes Wallis – a bouncing pass along the ground – to Gavin Hastings who collected, dummied Campo and went over for the try that put us in the lead. Gavin had spent much of the game worrying about whether he had taken a knock and ought to go off for treatment; he received scant sympathy from the rest of us and when he scored I think it put injury out of his mind too. From the kick-off everything went according to the textbook: we caught, Robert – reminiscent of Cardiff in the rain – kicked, Campo knocked on. Our scrum, Robert kicked, Campo was caught, we drove and released and Jerry put through his little grubber and followed up to score: 19–12. Two minutes later the whistle went.

That has to be one of the most memorable moments of my career. The sheer relief, the joy at having turned round the fortunes of the tour in a week. The grand slam is a longer drawn-out affair whereas in Australia we went from agony to ecstasy in a few short days. It was brilliant. Even better, we had the time to enjoy it because the tour schedule provided for a break of a week, part of it on Queensland's Gold Coast, before the third and deciding test back in Sydney. Everyone enjoyed the moment, even those in the stand, and we realised that we were back on course to take the series – which no Lions team had done since 1974 in South Africa.

It is a matter of history now that we won the third test 19–18 and that the series turned on a mistake David Campese made when trying to run a ball out from behind his own line. His pass inside to Greg Martin went to ground and Ieuan Evans got a hand on it first, the vital try which gave us the lead at 13–12. Gavin kicked two absolutely crucial penalties from long range and we hung on; even though Michael Lynagh made the difference only one point with his fourth penalty of the match, the Lions ended the stronger. When the whistle went we were only metres from their line and pressing, and our elation was plain to see. We did a lap of honour for the benefit of the travelling supporters and went off to enjoy ourselves.

In retrospect it was disappointing that the backs had not played a full part on the tour. The forwards developed into a magnificent unit but throughout the tour there was a lack of continuity; when you think about it, though, that final test was only the second time that XV had played together on tour, which underlines the difficulties of getting an effective side together on a short tour. So much work has to be done in the first place to bring together players of different styles from four countries; on the old Lions tour of 24 matches or longer, there was time to develop an effective pattern of play. That time is not available on a 12-match tour such as ours.

Now 12 matches may seem short compared with tours of years ago but in the modern world it is long enough. We have become accustomed to national tours of eight or nine matches, just over a month away from families and business, and players these days cannot afford much more time off to tour than that. As it was, when the Lions tour ended with the match against the ANZAC XV in Brisbane, I felt I had been a very long time away; I stopped off at Kuala Lumpur on the way home and met Wendy there so that we could take a holiday together. It was the first time she had been to Malaysia so I was able to show her some of the places I had called home; we visited the highlands in the interior and Wendy acquired a taste for the local food before we returned home and I took a break from rugby.

Such breaks do not last for long, though. England had a match against Fiji to prepare for in November and a knotty problem at centre – whether Jerry Guscott or Simon Halliday should play alongside Will in midfield. Jerry had begun his international career in something of an arrogant manner; he found it difficult to accept criticism or a spot of leg-pulling, and may have been a little insecure from that point of view. But he was selected ahead of Simon and that may have been a crucial stage in the maturing process, by increasing his confidence –

although the way he tells it, David Trick, the former England and Bath wing and a pretty laid-back character himself, made a comment one afternoon about Jerry's attitude problem which made him think very hard about it himself. I have roomed with him for much of the time since then when we meet for internationals and we get along fine.

Everyone reckoned that Rob Andrew came back from the Lions a much-improved player but having known him so long, with Yorkshire and the North, I have always believed he could command a game. He had not been doing so consistently at international level but on tour something clicked for him – whether it was Ian McGeechan's coaching, mixing with a lot of good players, having to challenge for the number one spot and the trust shown in him when he was given the test place so quickly I don't know, but he was a transformed player on the international stage.

The team to play Fiji was without several players from the previous season. Chris Oti and Dean Richards were both injured, Chris from the tour and Dean during Leicester's first league match at Wasps, and the selectors chose to try out two young props, Mark Linnett and Andy Mullins. They also recalled Richard Hill for his first international since 1987 but the nucleus of the Lions test side remained and public expectation was rewarded with a 58–23 win. Fiji had not enjoyed a good tour and we carved them up in the backs and although I scored five tries, I did not have a lot to do for most of them. Certainly I was not aware of existing try-scoring records – after all, I went into the match with the grand total of 13 from 33 games; I was miles behind Cyril Lowe's England record of 18.

One of the five involved a cut-back inside the cover and a final dash but the others were all straightforward run-ins. The one I regretted most was the one that Brian Stirling, the Irish referee, refused to award because he thought I had gone into touch but I still believe it was as good a try as any I have scored. Still, you can't complain about five tries in an international and to be told that I had equalled Lowe's mark, set back in the 1920s, was a very pleasant feeling. So I could scarcely claim to be upset that I had not broken it because of a disallowed sixth try!

That match set the tone for the Five Nations championship that season. We opened against Ireland at Twickenham and it took us the best part of an hour to find some kind of collective form. I had a mazy run early on but Keith Crossan covered back to stop me near the line and I tried to push the ball inside for Mickey Skinner who, to his great dismay, missed it; but Jeff Probyn took it on the half-volley and scored. Nevertheless we had to fight our way to a 13–0 lead deep in the second half before we started to find some space. Peter Winterbottom drew in the cover and Jerry broke through the middle before sending out a long pass to me and it was a case of pinning my ears back and going for the corner. As I started my dive I could feel someone around my legs but I had already got my push-off and I got the ball down.

That was the record. The television cameras showed how pleased I was but honestly I was happy just to have scored in the championship. Of the 18 tries I had scored for England until that match, only four had come in the championship and only two at Twickenham. Jerry rounded off a 23–0 win in his own inimitable manner and we were ready for Paris and what we regarded as the biggest test of the season; despite what everyone had written about that season, and the one that followed, we had made no fundamental decisions about playing 'open' rugby. What we looked for was quick ball, and against Ireland we didn't get it for an hour but we always felt that, against those particular opponents, we had the beating of them behind the scrum. We had looked to drive from line-outs and create choices, open or blind side, while from scrums we wanted a variety of back-row moves to suck in their backs and then move the ball wide. We were trying to recognise opportunities when they arose, so that when I scored my try, the situation cried out for the ball to be moved because the space was available. If the same situation had arisen in 1991, when people said we played a much tighter style, we would have done the same thing.

When we arrived in Paris we didn't run the ball that much, yet we came away with a 26–7 win and England's most emphatic performance against the French for years. It was a weird day at the Parc des Princes, the wind swirling around and the feeling of rain in the air, and although the pitch wasn't wet the ball was greasy. None of that seemed to make a difference to Simon Hodgkinson who kicked two brilliant penalties to give us an early lead, but it was from an unpromising position that I was able to score the first try. Hillie was under a lot of pressure when he shovelled the ball out to Rob who doubled back towards the right wing – my wing again that season, with Mark Bailey on the left – to see what was on. I shouted 'Kick it' to him and when I saw him shape to do so I put the pedal down. Patrice Lagisquet, my French counterpart, had come up too far and Serge Blanco was somewhere out on the open side and the kick was one of those which just goes your way. The ball bounced within a yard or so of the touchline and kept rolling and once I was past Lagisquet, all I could see was space. I could only pray that the ball would bounce right, but as I arrived it bounced off to the left and stopped about six inches from the try-line; I went for it and over the line in the same movement.

From that point England went away. The ball sat up kindly for Jerry to score a try too after he had kicked on, and the forwards had control up front with Mike Teague battering away from No 8. We led by 19–0 before France managed their seven points, including a try by Lagisquet when our drift defence did not function as planned. In an ideal world, such defence leaves the full-back without a man to tackle but Hodgie, mindful of Lagisquet's speed, said, 'I'll get up there and twat him.' In fact he came up at such a rate of knots that he crossed in front of me and checked the drift, leaving Lagisquet able to turn up the pace and cruise round the outside with the defence at sixes and sevens. Rob, hands on hips, looked at the three-quarters as though we were a bunch of naughty schoolboys but at that stage it didn't matter. We went back down the other end and Will finished off the scoring; none of us could believe it – a win by 19 points in Paris. It's hard to describe how good we felt about it.

We didn't feel too bad after we had played Wales, either. When the old enemy come to Twickenham the hype is not the same as for our visits to Cardiff but I felt I had something to prove after the disappointment of the previous year. I was back on the left wing with Hallers restored to the side on the right for a match in which the Welsh were given little chance. The first scrum of the match confirmed that view because they rattled backwards at a rate of knots; as soon as we saw that, we knew the likely outcome. As backs we frequently tell the forwards how good it makes us feel when we see them blowing the opposition away like that. Teaguie should have scored but knocked on; however Hodgie kicked a couple of goals and Will scored, again from a move which went slightly wrong because I had moved across to the right to support a forward drive going that way, and when Rob moved to the left he had only Will outside him. Will was committed, he handed off Mark Jones, a big No 8, as though he wasn't there, virtually ignored Mark Titley and then beat his way through Robert Jones's covering tackle to score in the corner. For strength and power you will see few better tries.

England's confidence by then was enormous. We felt anything was on and when Hillie and the back row gave me a sight of the corner, I was able to get past Mark Titley – who took a dreadful line on me – and over at the flag. I had to go somewhat further for my second try, which came when the Welsh dropped the ball in midfield on our 22 and I scooped it up to go all the way to the posts at the South end and dive over under the crossbar. I had been trying to throw off the effects of a cold all week and when Jerry came to pick me up I would have been happy enough to stay there, flat on my back! I walked back all the way and I was out, my head was just buzzing. The strict instruction went to Rob not to pass the ball to me.

There was a lot of good play in that game, more than in the previous two. As a side we were playing with enormous confidence, so that even though we had to go to Murrayfield for the final game against Scotland, we felt optimistic about the outcome. I hoped for the achievement of a personal ambition, to score in every game of a championship, and the way we were playing it seemed a possibility, even though the Scots themselves were unbeaten and had as much to play for as we did – grand slam, championship, triple crown, Calcutta Cup, the lot. The final training session at Peebles, the day before the match, was very sharp and enlivened by an RAF friend of mine who had better remain nameless overflying the pitch. He was flying from Lossiemouth and I told him where we would be, so when I saw a jet pass us about two miles to the south I thought he had missed us. Fifteen minutes later he had worked out where we were and, as we came off the training pitch, there was a thunderous roar and a Jaguar screamed over the valley. The postscript to that came when he landed and was passed a complaint from the Scottish Military who said that a man had fallen off a ladder in Peebles after a low-flying jet had given him a nasty shock. His exploit even made the Saturday morning papers: 'Possibly a friend of Rory Underwood's', the story read!

A lot has been made of the attitude with which England went into that grand-slam match. We were confident, yes, and we had reason to be but we all knew we still had to get out on the pitch and play the game. After it was over there was some comment that we had looked cocky running out at Murrayfield but it was exactly what we do every time; for all that, there is no doubt that the slow Scottish walk from the tunnel whipped up the crowd to a massive show of support. We certainly did not expect an easy match: I have never played against the Scots and had anything but a hard game. They are a very difficult side to play against and, on the day, pumped up as they were and tuned in to a game plan designed to stop the other side from performing, they did well. They were boosted by two early penalties, which gave them something to defend, but we scored a good try through Jerry from the one decent piece of second-phase ball we got all afternoon.

At that point we felt we were starting to play. For that reason I saw nothing strange in the forwards going for a pushover try when we camped down on their line and were awarded a series of penalties. I felt we had a slight domination up front and I knew how confident the forwards felt. Had it been the last quarter of the game with us trailing by two points, obviously the kick at goal would have been taken. I don't believe Will made the wrong decision at that time to go for a try; in the context of the game, and given the positive way we had been playing all through the championship, it seemed the natural way to play. Hindsight is a wonderful ally and people have argued that if Hodgie had kicked a penalty we would have won the game, but life isn't that easy; first he had to kick the points, in a tricky wind, and then we had to stay in front.

As it was we turned round 9–4 down but with considerable expectation, only to lose a try in that fatal period just after the interval. In fact the second half began well for us because Scotland kicked off into touch, giving us a scrum on halfway at which we called a move involving both wings. But Mike Teague knocked on, giving them the scrum, and they called a similar move off No 8 and scrum-half, with Gavin Hastings coming into a big right-hand field. Our defence was not spot on; I managed to push Gavin out towards the touchline but he kicked ahead and the bounce sat up nicely for Tony Stanger. At 13–4 down we threw everything at them and, I believe, played some very good rugby. But they tackled anything that moved and, at the end, we could not complain. The ball didn't run our way and the Scots played their hearts out; they took their chance, tactically they had worked out how to disrupt our game and they deserved to win.

The whistle sounded and the Scots went barmy. Why not? They had won. We walked back inside; people were sitting down, lying down, the dressing room was hushed. Defeat hurt. Eventually Will told us: 'Look, we're all disappointed but let's take on board what it feels like to lose a grand-slam game so that if we're in that position again we will know how hard it is to bear. We're not going to show people that we're down. We can go out and hold our heads high because we didn't disgrace ourselves.' It was not like the year before at Cardiff, when I had felt a personal responsibility. At Murrayfield we were not at our best as a team whereas the Scots were unity personified. As players it may be easier to come to terms with the fact of being beaten by a better team on the day than it is for the supporters, because we could not have tried harder; what it did do, of course, is provide extra motivation for, effectively, the same team over the next two years.

If we had won in 1990, I wonder if we would have done so well the following season and in the World Cup. We will never know the answer. At the time I was fortunate enough to have the immediate antidote because Wendy had won the Christmas draw at Cottesmore's air traffic control for which the prize was two tickets to Amsterdam or Paris. We flew out early on the Sunday from Edinburgh to London and then to Paris for a few days away from it all at the Officers' Club. It was brilliant. No English papers, no one recognised me and no one mentioned the match so I could let it recede and worry more about Wendy, who was six months pregnant. By the time we returned everything had settled down; the disappointment remained but the ache had departed. Mind you, a week or so later when we went to see Nigel Melville's daughter, Helen, who is our god-daughter, I was in a reception room when an old man wandered across and said, 'You didn't half spoil my Saturday the other weekend,' and wandered off again. There's not a lot you can say to that!

England were on tour that summer, in Argentina, but I had told Geoff Cooke at the beginning of the year I was not available. We were expecting our first child and I needed the time off from rugby. Rebecca made her appearance on 25 June, a day late; she was due on the Sunday but had not arrived by the time I went off on the Monday for the day's work. I was an instrument rating examiner and was flying in the afternoon but at 1 p.m. Wendy telephoned to complain of stomach cramps. Neither of us was certain of the best course of action but Wendy said she would be all right and I should stay on and fly. 'I've never done this before,' she added, perhaps unnecessarily! So I took off and kept flicking the radio back to Wyton's frequency in case anything should have happened. We completed the sortie, landed and I was just walking into the squadron when someone told me Wendy had gone into hospital.

I tore off my flying helmet and Mae West, threw them to the nearest colleague and screamed off up the A1 – inevitably I was stuck going through Grantham behind a cement mixer – arrived at the hospital and ran upstairs just in time to join in the birth. Cathy, a friend who is now Rebecca's godmother, had called round for a coffee just in time to run Wendy to the maternity unit but, having no children of her own, hadn't too much experience to call upon as Wendy went through her labour pains before being taken into the delivery room, where I was able to hold her hand as Rebecca made her appearance. That was a special moment, a very emotional moment. When Alexandra, our second, was born in December 1991, I was able to help with the delivery. If I had planned for something to put rugby into its proper perspective, I don't think I could have managed it any better.

11
Grand slam

There stands in the hallway of Annie Underwood's home in Barnard Castle a photograph of her eldest son, caught in the moment of triumph on 16 March 1991 when Les Peard had just blown the final whistle on England's match at Twickenham with France and the grand slam had been won. The photograph, blown up several sizes, depicts Rory leaping from the ground, arms aloft and the makings of a smile several miles wide which would last while the pitch was invaded (the crowd seized those of their heroes who were nearest and shouldered them off, Rory included), into the dressing room and deep into the evening.

It was the smile of a contented man at the end of a season which had become something of a personal crusade for the 1991 England XV. The same players went unchanged throughout the Five Nations championship, that unity confirming the conviction of those who had been there the longest that this, at last, was the season in which they would become winners. The chance had come twice before, and gone, and the players knew that it would not readily come again. In 1989 there was, at the least, a shared championship as the reward for victory over Wales in Cardiff. England lost. In 1990 the grand slam awaited the victor of the epic contest against Scotland at Murrayfield. England lost.

In 1991 everything was right for England: they had to play the weakest sides in the championship, Wales and Ireland, away from home and the Welsh were their first opponents so that nothing more hinged on the match than the result (ignoring, for a moment, the fact that England had not won in Cardiff since 1963, when several members of the 1991 side had not been born). The players the management required were available, with the sole exception of Chris Oti, the Wasps wing, who was still recovering from a ruptured Achilles tendon sustained while playing in an early-season sevens tournament. However, Nigel Heslop had taken advantage of the tour to Argentina in 1990 to win the confidence of both the management and, more importantly, his playing colleagues. It was the Underwood family's misfortune that he had done so at the expense of Tony, who had made the Argentinian tour but, troubled by lurking fitness problems, had not shown to best advantage.

The main problems the players faced were the organisation of commercial opportunities, following relaxation by the International Rugby Football Board of the amateur regulations, and the expectations of the press and public. In both respects it proved a difficult season but the playing hurdles were negotiated with style – if not the free-flowing style which had been evident during the 1990 championship. The pre-Christmas warm-up games against the Barbarians (won 18–16) and Argentina (won 51–0) had brought the vast majority of players back together and when the 1991 championship began, the Welsh citadel fell at last, booted over largely by Simon Hodgkinson who kicked seven penalty goals in the 25–6 victory.

Scotland followed at Twickenham with a similarly unromantic scoreline: 21–12 and another 17 points for Hodgkinson. In each match England scored one try; at the same stage of the 1990 championship they had scored seven tries but the overriding objective in 1991 was to ensure victory and if that meant pragmatism at the expense of entertainment then so be it. The quest resumed on 2 March at Lansdowne Road, never a ground where England have found life easy, and with eight minutes remaining they trailed 7–6; with seven minutes remaining they led 10–7 after one of the most valuable and individual tries of Rory's career. The final score of 16–7 won them the triple crown and a match at Twickenham against France who were also unbeaten. Just as at Murrayfield a year earlier, two sides met with everything to play for and England's winning margin of 21–19 was every bit as hard as the score suggests. France scored three tries to England's one, by Rory, and the first of their trio will go down as one of the great international tries, conceived by Serge Blanco behind his own line, brought to life by Didier Camberabero and scored by Philippe Saint-André. In the end it was Hodgkinson's goal-kicking which was critical to success and it earned the Nottingham full-back a Five Nations championship record aggregate of 60 points.

The main emotion I felt as the game against France ended was sheer relief that it was finally over. In the last couple of minutes of the game there had been only two points between us and any silly little error could have meant three points between the posts and we could have lost it. And for me it had been seven years of playing rugby for England; the year before we had missed out but this time we had done it.

I think I'm quite an emotional sort of character though I don't always show it. I tend to be the sort of person who is quiet, not terribly extrovert. And the moment of winning passed very quickly; the arms were up, I was looking for someone with whom to celebrate. Then I wanted to get off the pitch but by this time it was too late, the crowd was on the pitch and I was pushed up on someone's shoulders. For someone like me it was a bit embarrassing and all I wanted to do was get to the changing room and enjoy the moment with the lads. But once you are stuck up there there's nothing you can do. I saw Rob and the others there and everyone started to sing 'Swing Low Sweet Chariot' and you were enveloped in the atmosphere. Many times we've been mobbed going off the pitch but I think there must have been more people running on than normal. After all, the last time England had won a grand slam was in 1980, at Murrayfield when Billy Beaumont was carried off by his own players, and there must have been far fewer England supporters there that day. But I don't think I've heard so much spontaneous singing after the match and when one player was shouldered up, the rest just happened. It made the whole period of rejoicing immediately after the match seem much longer – particularly since it was so well captured on television – but a lot of what happened was unseen, in the changing room.

We all wanted to share the moment. That same XV had been together the season before, with only a few changes – Dean Richards had missed 1990 but he was an established part of the set-up so the only genuine newcomers were Nigel Heslop on the wing and Jason Leonard at prop. Both of them understood, having played in Argentina and during the early part of the season, what it meant to the rest of us. We had a point to prove and, having done so, we wanted to savour the moment. That's the thing that disappointed me, that by the time I got in there the initial euphoria had died down, and the feeling of anti-climax comes very quickly. I'll always remember it for my bit on the pitch but by the time we had got backstage, back to the hotel and changed for the dinner it was like any other post-match function.

It took a while to recover the moment later that night but when we did it was by far the most enjoyable evening I've had. Pretty well everyone stayed for the dance which follows the official banquet at the Hilton, and it was far better in consequence. Most of the team took over the bandstand: Deano was playing the drums with Jerry smashing the cymbals; I think Hallers was playing guitar, so was Dewi Morris. Some of the band got up and played to make it sound a bit better, then we started singing some Beatles numbers. It was a good night. But one of the worst things about international matches is that on Sunday mornings you all disperse. I went home to spend some time with the family and Monday morning I flew out to Hong Kong for a week with some of the RAF team to play in the ten-a-side tournament. I didn't even have the chance to get to work. You're back in your own, private world and it takes a little longer to sink in. I arrived back a week later to play for Leicester against Harlequins in a league match and all of a sudden I was back in the old routine.

To call it flat is a bit harsh but the spectator can review the impression of the whole game over and over, or on his video. We, the players, have lived the match second by second and when it's over we tend not to dwell on the past. You have the euphoria of the moment of winning, and that's what stands out. Yes, you've scored a try and other moments stand out too from the game but it doesn't linger quite so much for us as it might do for someone who has watched it all. As a player I see it not as a head-to-head with my opposite number but as a ruck here, a maul there, a kick to the corner, silly little things. Three months later, for instance, it's not a game that stands out in my mind as a whole.

I remember feeling that we had made a good start in the first ten minutes, then suddenly there was the try by Saint-André. That was a nine-pointer; instead of three points up from Simon's kick at goal we were six points down. Slowly we built up a good lead and I scored a try, but then the memory jumps to the last ten minutes of the game, when we weren't panicking but everyone was playing out of their skins to make sure the French did not come back and steal it. Curiously there was no great reaction among the team to Saint-André's try, because it was so early in the game; it was a magnificent score but we were thinking more of how we should have prevented it happening than anything else. We had decided that, against the French, the wingers wouldn't chase penalty kicks but would stay deep because the French like to take long drop-outs and it seemed pointless to chase the kicks then run 50 yards back for the drop-out. But we were lackadaisical in the pursuit of the kick and once the French had got through the first line of defence they were in their element. Camberabero was the one who made the try – chipping over me, catching the ball on the full and having the vision to see someone inside him half the width of the pitch away. It was tremendous. I don't think I have that kind of vision. I'd have been looking for the next man coming up behind me in support – and I can't kick as well as Camberabero anyway!

We were 6–3 down but we had been behind before in the championship, against Ireland, and we had enough experience, enough steel to fall behind and not let it worry us – unlike the England of old. The one side from whom it is difficult to recover the lead is Scotland – as we had found the year before at Murrayfield. But we had not lost to the French in the previous two seasons and at Twickenham there were no alarm bells. It was one of those tries that happened, there were mistakes and we changed our approach slightly, Nigel and I chasing penalty kicks and making sure the French could not run from their own line again because they had no space.

Even so it was level pegging at 9–9 when I scored the next try of the game. Basically it was a one-on-one, where you have your opponent directly opposite and as the ball comes to you, you check then go on the outside. It was a greasy day and as you take off you have a head start but you still expect the tackle, and Jean-Baptiste Lafond is no slouch in that respect. But I managed to get ahead of him and he slipped as he was coming in low; I managed to get a hand on his head to push him off with a few yards between me and the touchline. It wasn't the hardest try I've scored, not dissimilar to the one I had scored against Mark Titley in the Welsh match of the previous year.

They scored two tries in the second half, the first by Camberabero when the ball bounced their way. The kick came down right in front of me after Will and Dean collided in going for it and Camberabero was on it before I could move. Their third try was another outstanding individual score, by Mesnel, which made it 21–19, but I didn't feel even then that we could lose; we always knew we had to play for 80 minutes and deny them opportunities to score. As it turned out we established the lead and they had to play to beat us, which was a bit of a negative attitude but that's the way it was – just like the year before when we were the ones who had to play the rugby to beat Scotland, but their defence held. After all, we played remarkably well in that match, if a bit frantically, but there were some wonderful passing movements to look back on.

It's fair to say that our attitude going into the 1991 championships was bound up with what had happened the year before. We hadn't played the world's best rugby in 1989, even if we were in with a chance of the championships at the end of it, but in the 1990 season we had won three games, scored some cracking tries but lost the grand slam at the final hurdle. We knew we could win the grand slam but we had to make sure in 1991, control our own destiny.

There had been no great debate about our style of play at the start of the 1990–91 season. One of the features since Geoff Cooke took over as team manager has been that we take each game as it comes. We talked about the need for extra steel in our game but we never talked about 'the grand slam'. We played the warm-up games, against the Barbarians, against Argentina, then there was a gap for the divisional matches and when you are away for a couple of months there is always the need to reintroduce yourself to the other guys. When we went to Lanzarote for squad training in January the only thing in our minds was selection for the side to play Wales. We've always been a one-game-at-a-time team.

The Welsh game is always difficult because of the media interest, and now that we've broken the mould imposed since 1963, maybe it won't be the same again. The debate about the team's commercial aspirations only added to a difficult situation as the press hyped up the match, as they always do. It's not as though the squad was talking about potential business deals every five minutes. All we wanted to do was concentrate on the match in Cardiff, even though one or two squad members might have discussed some commercial aspects. And the idea that Will was involved all the time is entirely wrong; he has gone to great lengths to keep clear of it, because of his responsibilities as captain.

There was an additional complication for me because I was being quizzed by reporters about whether I might be flying in the Gulf. I decided to make a brief statement on my situation so as to lay the matter to rest but it didn't help my concentration. But far worse, when we had moved from Gloucester to Cardiff on the Thursday, was to switch on the television and see reports of bombing and rocket fire in Baghdad – so I knew that while I was preparing for a game of rugby, my service mates were at war.

That was underlined with awful weight on the Saturday morning; I came down to breakfast in the team hotel, opened a paper and saw the heavily bruised face of Flight Lieutenant John Peters staring out at me. John was on the junior course to mine at Cranwell and is a good friend of the family; now he was one of two airmen captured by the Iraqis after their aircraft had come down, and he looked, from the picture and judging by press reports, in a bad way. It completely unsettled me and I left the hotel and walked down the banks of the nearby River Taff, just for the chance to be alone and reflect. There were one or two curious remarks from local people passing by but I doubt if any of them knew what was running through my mind. The important thing was that John was alive and, happily, returned home when the war was over to resume his RAF career. But it puts sport into a different context altogether; there had already been some public questioning about the propriety of playing major representative games while we were at war but speaking to colleagues who served in the Gulf confirmed my opinion of the time, that the serving forces wanted the matches to go ahead, to give them something else to think about before they became embroiled in the fighting once more.

If the morning was a difficult time, so too was the evening after no English representative appeared at the post-match press conference. That decision was Geoff's. He had been pestered on the Friday and Saturday morning, woken up at all hours, and he had had a bellyful. From the strength of managing the winning side he decided against attending the press conference and he took the blame for it. Because of the whole backdrop to that particular match, it didn't take much for everyone to agree with the decision and I doubt if it would have happened at any other match.

Some of us – Wade Dooley, Peter Winterbottom, Rob Andrew – have been around a long time now and when we started, England's expectations scarcely amounted to more than a middle-of-the-table position from, perhaps, two wins against the weaker sides in the championships. We weren't very good. We tried our best and sometimes we were castigated. Now we have developed a side, the preparation has changed completely, and people expect us to win. They're surprised if we lose. But we still get castigated for the way we win. This winning lark is not all it's cracked up to be. I played for years and years in a mediocre England side. When I found myself playing in a successful side, and enjoying it, still people weren't happy. You wonder what it's all about, you really do. People criticised the way we won the grand slam, scoring only four tries, but at the end of the day that's what it's all about and in a couple of years' time people won't remember the style – they'll look back at our results and see 25–6, 21–12, 16–7 and 21–19 and they'll think, 'One close game but the rest seemed pretty clear wins'. Compare that with the Scotland side that won the 1990 grand slam – they nearly lost two of their games, their rugby didn't compare with some of the stuff we played but they didn't get any hassle for that.

I feel we don't get enough support from our press. I don't think people realise, except those who are very closely involved with the team, how much of a struggle it is against the hype that attends matches. After so many years of losing in Cardiff we went out and pushed them aside. A New Zealand team would have done no different; if all those penalties had come up Grant Fox would have put them over, just as Simon Hodgkinson did for us. On a dry day it could have been different but it was greasy and if you have someone of Simon's kicking calibre in the side, you don't think twice about putting him on. Especially when he's not missing them. We had only one thing in mind in Cardiff: to win. I felt good about coming off the field, having done the job we set out to do. In the changing room there was just quiet satisfaction, nothing more, none of the cracks from the players who tend to whoop it up a bit after a good victory. It was the first match of the championship and we were relieved the bogey had been shoved out of the window; all we wanted to do was to get out of Cardiff and look ahead.

We had changed our preparation for that match by staying in the city centre itself rather than remaining outside, at Chepstow for example. Will wanted the change. He asked several people and the general consensus was 'yes'. I agreed although I had a few reservations and I still can't say whether or not it was right. To me it didn't make a lot of difference psychologically, though it may have done for some of the others. And one of the great elements in this side is the way we talk to each other, the amount of communication that goes on, both in training and during matches. Geoff has always emphasised that he wants everything to come from us.

Not that we needed to talk a great deal about the second game of the championship, against Scotland. We needed to win to make up for what had happened the previous season. We know the Scottish game well, we have suffered before; they thrive on opponents' mistakes, but in addition our forwards felt they had not played anywhere near their best in 1990. They had a big point to prove and they did, especially in the loose. In fact, Gary Armstrong apart, the Scots in 1991 did not offer any threat at all and although we scored only the one try against them, it did typify the sort of rugby we could play and had played so well the season before. In that respect, though, I'm a great believer in the theory that you always get caught in your second season; in 1990 we had played some fabulous rugby so in 1991 people were looking out for us, trying to mark us out of the game.

The Scots tend to play a spoiling game anyway – I've never been in an England side that has beaten them convincingly. The best we have managed in my time was the 21–12 game in 1987 when Marcus Rose scored 17 points and although I've recorded good wins home and away against all the other countries in the Five Nations championship, it has never happened against the Scots. Again it was a case of relief that we had won, that we had settled the account for 1990. It was difficult for us to play an expansive game; in 1990 we had thrived on second- and third-phase ball which we had spun wide, but the Scots have made an art form of getting into positions where it is difficult for their opponents to win possession.

None the less it was two down with two to go, but no one was coming out with any predictions about the championship as a whole. The public, certainly the media, were starting to make expectant noises but we were trying to keep events in perspective; we have had the experience of being built up only to be knocked down.

We knew we had to go to Lansdowne Road and play the Irish. At Twickenham it's a different matter but the first ruck, the first high ball in Dublin and all you can see is whirling dervishes wearing green shirts. That young Irish side, in our third match, with nothing to lose against a well-fancied England side, came out with all guns firing. We felt we could exploit their backs but on the day the weather was indifferent and their forwards played out of their skins and won far more ball than most people expected.

It was billed as the triple crown match, of course, which may mean something to a lot of players but doesn't register much with me. The modern player is looking at a four-game championship. The triple crown may have been the big thing before France joined, or before they had established a meaningful presence – which effectively means after the Second World War. I find it strange that England, or Scotland in 1990 for that matter, should be described as the side that won the grand slam, triple crown and Calcutta Cup. The grand slam says everything. If I won the triple crown and lost the grand slam I'd be well hacked off.

At Lansdowne Road I came face to face with Simon Geoghegan, who was possibly the discovery of the 1991 championship. I had seen something of him and he struck me as a powerful lad though not that powerfully built, tallish but not quite in the John Kirwan mould. But I don't tend consciously to dissect the other wing – maybe sub-consciously I'm frightened about the effect it will have on my game – although even when I was young I didn't. I won my first cap against Trevor Ringland, whom I knew because I had played for Yorkshire against Ulster; similarly I knew Keith Crossan, Clive Rees and Keith Robertson, who were the wings around in the other countries in 1984. I was aware of joining an elite band but I already knew most of them anyway. I tend not to think too much of what they might do but go out intent on playing my own game, doing my own job as well as I can.

Having said that, Geoghegan scored a try against me just after half-time, which is the period when England are aware of a certain vulnerability. We lost the 1990 Scotland game to a try just after the interval and the same happened in the 1989 Wales game in Cardiff when, for some reason, they kicked off long to me and I knocked it on to concede a scrum from which the winning try developed. It's happened so often that one of the things Will always says after the half-time huddle breaks up is, 'Play well for the next ten minutes, make sure they don't get in.'

On this occasion Geoghegan was less than ten yards from our line, on their scrum feed. The blind side was too narrow for Hodgie to come across so he stayed on the open side and the back row stayed down to prevent any possibility of a pushover. That left me exposed to a straight one-on-one on the wing, when the player with the ball in his hands has the initiative. I tackled him, and he swung into touch but managed to get the ball down before his legs hit touch. There was no dispute about it among the team but another black mark against that particular corner of Lansdowne Road where I have had two other international tries scored against me. One was by Trevor Ringland, when I actually stopped him but Deano, covering across, came in with a tackle and knocked me off balance, pushing Trevor back over the line; the other was a peel round the front of the line-out by Phil Matthews when I did a cracking tackle on him but so low that he went over the top and scored.

But on this occasion the fact that my opposite number had scored didn't worry me unduly. In 1989, when I contributed rather too much to the try Wales scored – which effectively won the game – it was a big psychological blow which lingered with me for some time. Geoghegan's try was a situation in which I did my best, but he did slightly better and he deserves the credit for it. The other England players shrugged their shoulders and got on with the job of winning the match, which is a reflection of the backbone that had developed in that team. And as it happened I was able to get the try back; it was good to even the score but that it should have been so valuable a try made it even better.

It was the second time we had gone down that side but the ball hadn't run to me. The first time Will decided to go on his own but this time there was still a lot of cover around – two against two with their full-back, Jim Staples, behind. We were playing a relatively tight game and I made the decision to go for the scissors with Hodgie;

immediately I received the ball I found someone in front of me so I sidestepped to the left and half-handed him off and in the process found myself going through a gap back to the left. That had the effect of wrong-footing Geoghegan who was coming across and by this time Hodgie had come up on the outside. I could see Crossan coming across and in my mind I was going to pass but out of the corner of my eye I could see Hodgie and thought he was too deep, so I checked and went out again. Looking at the video afterwards I still don't know why Keith didn't get a good tackle on me; as he hit me I thought I had made the wrong decision but then he came off and my only thought was to get that ball down over the line.

That was a huge blow to the Irish. They were against the wall anyway, possession had dried up but their defence was so good that they must have hoped they could hang on to their one-point lead. We weren't getting too anxious, though; we avoided falling into the same trap that we had at Murrayfield the year before when we kept battering away without reward, but there was a touch of the headless chickens in what we were doing. We weren't that conscious of the time factor in Dublin, even though when I scored there were only seven minutes left. We were pressing them all the time, we were in control. The final score didn't reflect the extent of that control.

Every Irishman I have ever played against has been a great sportsman, on and off the field. When we lost to them 17–0 in 1987 they were exactly the same as when we beat them 35–3 a year later. We could probably have done without some of the remarks that Rob Saunders, then Ireland's captain, came out with after the game, which slightly soured the evening, but he was young and inexperienced which might explain it. But even so it was a good night in Dublin, as it always is. The triple crown was won but no one was celebrating unduly. We had the satisfaction of the victory and the relief of knowing that we had played, we hoped, our one bad game of the season and got away with it. Security in Dublin demands that the visitors are away from the dinner around 11 p.m. and back at their own hotel – though some of the back-row players usually manage to find their way to one of the local pubs. The players' wives were over too, so we were all able to make a decent weekend of it because our flight on Sunday didn't leave until mid-afternoon, so everyone pitched up for Sunday brunch at the team hotel.

The arrangements were exactly the same as they had been all season for the decisive match with France. We realised after the Irish game that there were some questions still to be answered – the scrummaging

had not been that hot, it was not until the last quarter that Dean and
Mike Teague had been able to start sorting out the Irish, some of the
back movements had gone across the field. It was a matter of
tightening the nuts and bolts of our game. We had hoped to exploit the
inexperience in the Irish back division – Brendan Mullin apart – but
the weather conditions, wet and slippery, weren't conducive to
running rugby. We were not about to change tactically. When we play
France we tend to target certain players – Blanco at full-back, Berbizier
at scrum-half, but no forwards on this occasion. In other years it
would have been Laurent Rodriguez and Daniel Dubroca but the year
before, in Paris, we had destroyed them and in particular Berbizier
who has been the linchpin to everything they do.

The mood in the team hotel at Richmond before the game was tense,
although I'm lucky in that respect, I don't tend to get nervous before a
game. The heart flutters a bit when we have the team meeting because
we are all focusing in, but thereafter the routine takes over: on the bus,
into the ground, through the crowd, on to the pitch, back to the
changing room, and I'm fine. The crowd when we arrived at
Twickenham was the biggest yet; there was a line of people all the way
from the bus to the players' entrance under the West Stand, a tunnel of
people leading us in. The worst thing about the day was waking in the
morning, looking out of the window and seeing the drizzle. That was a
dampener (excuse the pun) especially for the backs; the conditions in
Paris the year before had not been wonderful but the ball was not wet
and we had moved it around.

The rest of the day, though, just got better and better. The
atmosphere was marvellous, during the match and afterwards. In the
end it made the seven years of trying worthwhile.

12

On top of the world – nearly

When the first World Cup tournament was played in 1987, few countries had made significant preparations specifically for the tournament and New Zealand, with a strong playing base – in quality if not quantity – with home advantage and with several of the better coaching and conditioning brains available in world rugby, won. The northern-hemisphere countries, France excepted, had made little impact on the tournament, but in 1991 they were determined to do better.

England, in particular, were conscious of their failings in 1987 and much of what had happened subsequently had been aimed directly at success in the 1991 competition. The 1990 tour to Argentina was not part of the preparation but had been proffered to the Argentine federation by the late John Kendall-Carpenter, in his role as chairman of Rugby World Cup. In contrast the Rugby Football Union wanted a harder tour in the summer of 1991 to keep the national squad in good order. Their plans to tour Australia and Fiji did not meet with universal approval: it was not, the critics said, the time to make such a demanding trip and risk morale-sapping defeat, nor could the players be expected to sustain their level of fitness throughout the summer and up to the date of the World Cup final in November.

While the players were preparing for their summer excursion, however, the World Cup bandwagon was the subject of intense scrutiny. The logistics of the tournament were about as complicated as they could be; despite the recommendations of the organising committee back in 1987, that it should be played in one country, the tournament had been divided among the four home unions and France, bringing into play three different legal systems – which affected some of the commercial negotiations – different languages and currencies, different television and radio requirements. The Rugby Football Union had offered at an early stage to host the tournament but had been turned down. However, all five host unions

*appointed their individual World Cup officers and all took part in the
message relay: the running of a rugby ball from Rugby School up and
down the British Isles, Ireland and France so as to advertise the
tournament and attract youngsters to the game.*

*The tournament was the biggest to take place in Britain since the
football World Cup of 1966 and was recognised as an immense
marketing opportunity for the game. The players, naturally enough,
were part of that opportunity. The England squad, adopting their own
commercial advisers, worked out a promotional campaign called 'Run
with the Ball' which was linked to the World Cup; the national squads
of Scotland, Ireland and Wales were all investigating opportunities in
the same area in the light of relaxation of rugby union's amateur
regulations, permitting players to make money from off-the-field
activities not directly connected with the game.*

In 1990 all the players in the England squad had been given a wall
chart. It outlined in graphic detail the two-year plan which we had to
follow if we were to take part in the 1991 World Cup and was a
constant reminder of how much rugby was eating into our daily
existence. The focus of the chart was England's game against New
Zealand at Twickenham on 3 October, the opening game of the
tournament, and it told us what levels of fitness should be achieved,
what peaks we should be hitting, when we could relax training and
when we could step it up.

Everybody knew what was involved if we were to do well in the
World Cup, let alone win it. The training was hard, the tour of
Australia was hard and then there were three games in September to
keep us in trim for the tournament itself. For amateur players, with
daily jobs to sustain, it was a massive commitment of time and effort,
of absence from the work place, from families. Looking back it seems
even harder than it appeared at the time but we accepted it as necessary
if we were to compete with the southern-hemisphere countries who
were seen as the pre-tournament favourites.

We had all become accustomed to receiving periodic reports on our
fitness from Rex Hazeldine from Loughborough University's Depart-
ment of Physical Education and Sports Science. Fitness checks were
built into the rolling programme and it was Rex's job to spot specific
areas on which we needed to work; I received a daunting memo in June
just before the tour which said: 'Your body fat has increased to 13.6
per cent and although it is still well within the range of 12–15 per cent,
you need to carefully watch your diet (high carbohydrate, low fat) and

with the increased training over the next two months, this value will come down again.'

At the same time Rex emphasised by his figures that the Australian tour was only a step on the road to the peak in the autumn. 'You've maintained your flexibility well but your strength is a little below average for the backs,' his memo continued. 'Your speed is another area where, with the appropriate work now, you look set to be your best ever before the [World] Cup . . . . We suggest you use the tour to work on speed over shorter distances, and power. When you return in August you can work on extending your speed over longer distances. Remember to include some endurance work on tour at the appropriate opportunity.'

No rest for the wicked! This is only a small example of the attention to detail which is nowadays paid to the England squad, and to which I believe the Australians and the New Zealanders have become accustomed, thanks to the work of the Australian Institute of Sport and, in New Zealand, the work of Jim Blair, the fitness adviser. Rex's final letter, just before the World Cup, read: 'With very few exceptions the fitness levels of the squad are at, or above, the targets that were aimed for at this stage. The hard work has been done, fitness-wise, so make sure you don't over-train over the next few weeks [no chance of that] and hide your true fitness with fatigue . . . . It's quality rather than quantity of training that counts at this stage.'

Broadly speaking the planning for 1991 had been worked out by Geoff Cooke, in concert with Don Rutherford, the RFU's technical administrator. Several players grumbled about touring so soon before the tournament while others thought it was the right thing to do – which probably reflected what many observers thought. I had reservations initially about so hectic a schedule before a World Cup but the benefits of going away together for a month, of eating and sleeping rugby, could do nothing but bring us together as a squad; the one factor we had to guard against was staleness, and a lot of work was put into ensuring that entertainments were provided during our spare time so that there was some relief from rugby.

But the fact that it had to be a graduated tour worked against the natural desire to beat Australia – which, as has been heavily underlined, was a feat England had never achieved in Australia. We were all aware from the outset that our fitness levels were not at their highest; we had reached a peak during the winning of the grand slam and while we had kept playing club rugby, we had retreated from that peak because the important time to rediscover it was in the autumn, not the summer. In the event we returned from the tour with a record of won three, lost four, which does not sound impressive and was made worse by the scale of the 40–15 defeat by Australia – but with hindsight I believe it was the best thing we could have done.

It showed how good the Australians were and posed a lot of questions for any England team which fancied its chances of winning the World Cup. We toured in a spirit of exploration, to examine a variety of playing avenues to see if they would improve our overall game; this is a natural development in any squad which comes together at regular intervals and consists largely of the same personnel. There is frequent discussion of tactics, particularly the morning after a game, of what worked, of what didn't work and why. On tour everyone has the chance to express their opinions and to suggest areas of improvement and one of the first quandaries which had to be resolved was the absence of Simon Hodgkinson, who had been so influential in the winning of the grand slam because of his goal-kicking. Simon began the tour as first-choice full-back but suffered a nasty bang on the nose in training, which seemed to unsettle him and affect his confidence.

He missed the opening game, against New South Wales, when England lost 21–19 but which we did not regard as a disaster given the strength of the opposition, the prolonged preparation they had had and the fact that we were only a few days off the aircraft which brought us from England. And one man's misfortune is another man's blessing; Jonathan Webb, who had played in the 1987 World Cup and is a very talented performer, stepped up and played well, well enough to keep Hodgie out.

None the less the fact remained that, passing the halfway stage of the tour, we had won one and lost three games. Queensland won 20–14 and scored three tries from set pieces – two of them from five-metre scrums which was disappointing for the back row – and even more disappointing was the 27–13 defeat against Fiji B in Laotoka. I don't think morale was really low but it was certainly tested and it was a testimony to the character of the squad that we did not retreat to the situation which was apparent on tour in Australia in 1988, when one group blamed another for the way the tour was going. There was no dissension in 1991 but a quiet acceptance that things had gone wrong and we would have to knuckle down and work harder.

Those of us who had played for the Lions in Australia in 1989 were surprised by how much the Australians had improved. New South Wales and Queensland were both good sides but defeat in the first of the two games in Fiji was not on the cards; in the first half of that match England played quite well but there were some unusual refereeing decisions in the second half by Laiakini Colati – who was one of the World Cup panel referees – and we had to admit that the back line was not functioning properly. In addition there had been some important injuries: John Hall was struggling with an old knee injury and eventually returned home early; Wade Dooley broke a bone in his hand against Queensland which ruled him out; and both Paul Ackford and Peter Winterbottom were carrying injuries in Fiji.

It all served to put a lot of pressure on us going into the first international, against Fiji in Suva. Anyone who has played there knows how hard it is to do well – not many national sides from Australia and New Zealand go visiting – yet England have played there whenever the opportunity has arisen and have won. We were without both the locks who had played so well together since 1988, Ackers and Wade, and Martin Bayfield came in for his first cap, alongside Nigel Redman, which meant the pack having to integrate in difficult circumstances. For the first 60 minutes Fiji knocked us around but, with a touch of naivety, didn't capitalise and kicked a lot of possession away. We came with a late surge and were relieved to run out with a 28–12 win.

We desperately needed it, to lift the party before the game with Australia a week later, and Martin's form was very encouraging. Rob Andrew was a happy boy too: he scored his first try for England – in his 37th international – although we all reckoned it had to be the shortest try in the game! He followed a chip through by Jerry Guscott which beat the defence and Chris Oti and Rob scooped it up on the line and went over.

A week later and a different story. Australia left the Sydney Football Stadium with the cheers of the crowd ringing in their ears after their biggest victory over England, by 40–15. It was one of those days that we have all enjoyed at some stage, when everything you try works; it's not necessarily that the other side is bad or having a poor day, but simply that every decision made proves to be the correct one, and in a team game like rugby that does not occur all that often. During the game itself none of us felt that we were being thrashed to the extent the scoreline suggests. We had a lot of possession but, running from deep as we did so often, we couldn't score; against that the Australians, whenever they reached our 22, seemed to score which obviously posed questions about our defence and, in particular, the back row which was felt to be a bit slow. We pride ourselves on back-row and blind-side defence but here of their five tries, two were scored by Willie Ofahengaue, their blind-side flanker, and one from a back-row/ scrum-half move by David Campese. We could not complain that we had not been warned because Queensland had scored two soft tries close to the scrum. And this was our first experience of Willie O; he played against us for New South Wales, but in his first international he was tremendous and so difficult to pull down once he had got into gear.

In the post mortem, in the hotel afterwards and on the flight home, there was general agreement that the tour had served a useful purpose. We had set out as the bees' knees, having just won the grand slam; we were looking forward to touring, working out a few variations before returning home and giving the World Cup our best shot. But having arrived in Australia, all of a sudden we were working very hard just to keep up in provincial matches and discovering how the Australians had moved ahead since 1988–89. The Aussies had already beaten New Zealand (and were to do so again a month later) and the All Blacks were our first World Cup opponents. The tour gave us a yardstick of what we had to achieve in the next two months if we were to have a chance of winning the World Cup. We never managed to win as much line-out ball as we had hoped, and the scrummaging was not as solid as we would have liked; the virtues that had helped us to the grand slam were no longer there.

We had been brought down to earth with a thud. But the response was not dramatic change because we were only two months away from the World Cup; instead we looked at specific aspects of England's game and tried to improve or correct them. We also looked at the opposition for areas of weakness to exploit; but our main failure was the inability to score when we reached opposing 22s; our record in that respect is pathetic. We were given a clinical lesson by the Australians and even now we are still trying to achieve their standard of strike-rate.

Our first opportunity to put what we had learned into practice came in the three warm-up games which preceded the World Cup, against the Soviet Union – just before the Soviet Union ceased to exist – Gloucester and the England Students. They were a very useful series of games, bringing us together again so that we could focus on the demands we faced in October; it didn't matter that they were not particularly demanding games because they gave us the chance to get used to the knocks and to practise the moves we hoped to use. It was not a case of trying to prepare for the specific style of the All Blacks –

that would have been asking a bit much, even of Gloucester – but of working on our game.

At that stage the World Cup didn't seem to have impinged to a great extent on the British public. The squad had worked out some commercial opportunities off the field but they, too, were in abeyance until the International Rugby Football Board ruled that the promotional Run with the Ball scheme came within the amateur regulations. The arrangements for promoting the game were in place, organised with the help of the Rugby Football Union development officers, but at that stage we did not know whether it would mean anything at all in financial terms. The media interest had yet to build up, either in the papers or on television, and I wouldn't have thought the layman knew much about the forthcoming tournament.

In my opinion the World Cup did not really hit the public consciousness until we qualified to play France in the quarter-finals. Suddenly it was Agincourt and Waterloo rolled into one. But you have to remember that, until then, the squad was isolated; we came together for the warm-up games and departed back to our respective homes and jobs until all the teams gathered in late September, met briefly for the pre-tournament dinner and then went into retreat – in our case to Tylney Hall near Basingstoke in Hampshire. That in itself was not a popular move with the World Cup organising committee, who had allocated a hotel in London only to find that the Rugby Football Union had made other arrangements because we wanted to be out in the country, not near London with all its distractions. There were various grumbles about that, as there were when we went off to the Channel Islands in mid-tournament and then stayed a couple of nights in the Belton Woods Hotel and Country Club just outside Grantham in between the semi-final and the final.

The RFU did well for us there. Tylney Hall, set in its own land, provided lovely surroundings and though one or two of the forwards said they were bored, I thought it was excellent. There was a golf course attached, clay-pigeon shooting if we wanted – in fact, anything we wanted was provided, cars as required, videos in individual rooms, newspapers in the team room; Will Carling, understandably, was very peeved when people complained that there wasn't enough to do. The management was happy to organise anything, except that those who complained seemed to have no clear idea of what they did want – although I dare say there was an element of being on tour in our own country which the Australians had found frustrating in 1987.

Day one of the tournament proper was 25 September when we

made our own way down to Hampshire from Richmond. We had already met one of our sponsors' engagements the previous day, attending a dinner with Courage, the brewers who back the league championship in England. Adjourning to our regular hotel, the Petersham, we collected the leisure gear made available from Cotton Traders, the firm who had been awarded the contract to supply a controversial World Cup strip for England – controversial because it departed from the traditional all-white and introduced red and blue stripes on the sleeve and coloured flashes at the collar and on the cuffs. I could understand the traditionalists who regretted the departure but I had no qualms about the new jerseys; I think it was an issue which troubled observers more than it did the players.

Having attended to the preliminaries we drove down the M3, attended by thunder and lightning, to Basingstoke. We were able to make ourselves thoroughly at home with a golf day at the local club and training began on the Saturday, six days before the opening of the tournament; the same day, though, we had to drive back up to the centre of London for the World Cup welcoming dinner for which, in common with most players, I could not see the need. I suppose the organisers enjoy parading the players of 16 nations before the sponsors, administrators and guests who attend the dinner but few of the players sought the welcome, particularly those who had to come from a distance like the Irish and the French – who were distinctly unimpressed and left for home as soon as they decently could. The teams were split, with the idea that you should not be sitting with another team from your pool, but the Irish found themselves warily eying the Zimbabweans, whom they were due to play first.

The minds of all the players were turned inwards for probably the most significant moment of their sporting lives. They wanted their own company, not that of others and far less that of their opponents during the coming weeks. So we dispersed to our respective training camps – while we were at Basingstoke the All Blacks were at Weybridge, the Australians disappeared down to Wales, and the Americans and the Italians (the other two countries in our pool) went north to Leeds. Our preparations included a training morning with local youngsters at Basingstoke Rugby Club, where the local officials worked very hard to make a success of our stay, but there comes a time when all you want is for the first match to come and the show to get on the road.

Come it did on a damp 3 October. Prince Edward read to a hushed Twickenham the World Cup message, which a month earlier I had helped on its way round the British Isles in my Hawk, representatives of each competing country paraded, Michael Ball sang the World Cup song (like us he came second too, in the Eurovision Song contest six months later!) and we were off. Not that we, as players, saw any of that. In our dressing room we were concentrating on the game, the first time that most of us – Wade, Teaguie and Winters were exceptions – had played in a national team against New Zealand. But their experience was six or eight years old and video analysis had played the major part in our preparations.

We knew what to expect, we knew how we wanted to play, we had been waiting for the moment for two years – and we lost. It had been such a big build-up that the disappointment, inevitably, was all the greater. Yet it was an education in how to control a game. New Zealand adapted far more quickly to the circumstances of the day, they were never rattled by going behind 12–9 at the interval and they ran out 18–12 winners. Some overture. Yet we were in with a chance and one of the things we talked about afterwards was how well the Blacks had lifted the pace of the game in the second half. I was not so aware of it on the wing but the forwards certainly felt it. Not only did New Zealand control the tempo of the game, they controlled the ball and we, as backs, had little opportunity. One try, by Michael Jones, and conversion made the difference in the end.

We had the better part of a week to contemplate the blow to our expectations. We had hardly looked beyond that game, such was the extent to which it had dominated our preparations. We were aware, of course, that we could still qualify by beating Italy and the USA and that, if we did, we had beaten within the last six months the opponents we were likely to face, France and Scotland. But it took an effort to focus our thoughts on the next two opponents and the major pick-me-up the management could offer was that there was still every prospect of reaching the final.

And, in case anyone was still brooding, we had a busy weekend scheduled. After a light training session on the Friday morning we flew to Leeds and travelled over to Harrogate, for a civic dinner in the evening, a coaching morning with local youngsters at the rugby club and then to watch our next opponents play each other at Otley. Not that we left the All Blacks game entirely alone; before the dinner in Harrogate backs and forwards sat down together to talk it over, in particular defence down the left-hand side of the field which is where they had scored their try.

Talking, though, could not bring back the moment and we had to look ahead. After a thorough Yorkshire soaking at Claro Road, when the rain sheeted down as we coached a horde of youngsters, the sun came out in time for the Italians' 30–9 win over the USA and we returned to London that evening reflecting on the elusive running of Ivan Francescato, their scrum-half, and the goal-kicking of Diego Dominguez. Not that, when we came to play Italy, either half-back had much opportunity to display his skills in a game ruined by the Italians' abuse of the offside laws; Brian Anderson, the experienced Scot who refereed the game, had little option but to penalise them throughout because they kept killing the ball. They were struggling in the set pieces and obviously they felt they had to stop us playing, and to an extent they succeeded because there was no flow or continuity to the game. But it was good to open our account and score some tries, four in all including one for Webbie who returned a record haul of 24 points (four penalties, four conversions).

Meanwhile the Americans emerged from their pool game against New Zealand with considerable credit and it was already apparent that the All Blacks, for all their win against us, were not performing to peak efficiency – the Italians underlined that when they held them to a ten-point margin in the final pool game. You could argue, too, that we were not over-impressive against the USA even though there was never any doubt who would win. Admittedly we changed the side a lot for that match, to give everyone else in the squad a game, with the exception of the reserve half-backs, Dewi Morris and David Pears. Geoff Cooke had decided early on that the key decision-makers, Richard Hill and Rob Andrew, would probably play all the games, which brought back memories of the 1987 World Cup when we played the same back row throughout the pool games and by the time we arrived at the quarter-final against Wales, they were worn out.

Whether it was the correct decision is hard to say. Since we got through to the final you could argue that Geoff was right and the further we progressed, the more important each game became and the more unlikely it was that Dewi and Pearsie would play. As far as the game against the USA was concerned a lot of changes had been made elsewhere and it was felt that we should retain stability in that key area. The end product was by no means a thrilling performance but it was solid enough for us to win 37–9 and thus qualify for the knockout stage of the tournament, in Paris against France who had emerged unbeaten from their pool, which included Fiji, Romania and Canada.

We also earned ourselves a mid-tournament break in Jersey, which the RFU had organised for the players and their wives – and pushed past the complaints of the World Cup organisers by arguing that Jersey was part of Hampshire (they are placed in that county in the Courage Clubs Championship)! I was really disappointed that Wendy could not travel but she was six months pregnant with Alexandra and not allowed to fly. The wives and girlfriends who did come, though, had a tremendous time and we could all relax, play golf – Jerry and I were able to play the championship course at La Moye – and go for walks. Brian Moore and I missed the first night there because we had agreed to appear on the *Motormouth* television show but rumour has it that the relaxation on the Friday evening had to be seen to be believed and even Winters was distinctly wobbly as the night wore on. It was all captured on video, too, and shown to the squad before the game with Wales later in the season – it's a wonder we still won the grand slam!

It was a wonderful opportunity for everyone to let their hair down and all credit to the RFU for arranging it. The serious business lay ahead, though. We had kept in touch with the action in the other pools, like any other enthusiast by watching what appeared on television. The keenest interest, obviously, was in the French whom we always expected to play, and anything else tended to be optional; a wary eye was kept on the All Blacks who were not playing as well as expected, but as the pool games developed my money was drifting towards Australia to make it through to the final. The Western Samoans impressed everyone with their tackling and we were happy to see them emerge as quarter-finalists against Scotland because we felt they would take quite a lot out of the Scots – whom, if all went well, we were likely to meet in the semi-finals.

Before that, though, the team management faced some difficult decisions in selection. Chris Oti had been upset at missing John Kirwan in our opening game, which gave New Zealand their try, and in the following game, with Italy, he and I swapped sides with the idea of shoring up defence on the left-hand side while Chris matched up to Geoff Cooke's perception of right-wing play, which has to do with strength and power and who can set up play for the back row, whose moves mostly go right. That's why Geoff likes playing Simon Halliday on the right and, before him, John Bentley, both of whom are centres by trade.

Meanwhile Nigel Heslop had waited patiently for his chance. Nigel played in the 1991 grand slam, when Chris wasn't fit, but lost his place on tour in Australia without having done anything wrong. I felt sorry for Nige but he played well against the USA, scored a neat try and when it came to the French game it was a straight choice and he won the place.

But the major change was at No 8 where Dean Richards was omitted and Mike Teague moved across from blind-side flanker, leaving a vacancy for Mickey Skinner. Deano has been a major figure in English rugby but the feeling at the time, certainly among the backs, was that the back row wasn't quick enough. I had a talk with Geoff about it, as did some of the other senior players, and expressed the view that, for the French game particularly, we needed more pace from the back row. Geoff listened, as he always does, then went away, talked with Roger Uttley and made the decision. Dean took it as you would expect, with great fortitude; whether it made the difference between winning and losing I don't know but it improved our play, because it was our best game of the tournament. Our defence was exceptional, so was our discipline and the way we were able to clear our lines.

It was one of the hardest games I have ever played in. In the days immediately before the game, the pressures of the competition began to take effect because we all realised that if we lost on the Saturday we would be back at work on the Monday; the knockout stage concentrates the mind wonderfully. Our first training session in France provoked some headlines because of the intensity of the tackling and of the forward play, but that was deliberate and there was certainly no animosity, whatever may have appeared in the papers. We had talked in Jersey about players not being quite as focused on the match as the management wanted, and picked two sides to play 'for real' against each other in training. It was as though a switch had been clicked and the atmosphere and attitude after that session were just right and were a large part of the reason for our winning.

The match itself started with a flurry, of course, when Nigel followed a high ball and caught Serge Blanco slightly late, which provoked a hail of blows on Nigel from Blanco and others. Maybe that said something about French nerves but I found the whole atmosphere stimulating, as always, and by no means hostile. We were aware of the volume of support, too, and they had something to cheer when Blanco was penalised for punching by David Bishop, the New Zealand referee, and Webbie kicked the goal.

By half-time we led 10–6; another penalty from Webbie and Jerry set up a try for me, against two close-range penalties by Thierry Lacroix. But in the third quarter we came under tremendous pressure and the performance in defence was the best I can remember. I was right beside

Skins when he put in a tackle on Marc Cecillon which has gone down in history as one of the genuinely big hits. France levelled when a high ball cannoned off Webbie's shoulder and Lafond worked his way round Nigel for a try, but then came a period of stalemate, of the long kicking to and fro which has not helped make the game more attractive as a spectacle and which the International Board has now taken steps to limit.

Yet, in the end, that game helped towards a score. Webbie had given us back the lead after indiscipline by Pascal Ondarts, and then Olivier Roumat, one of their better players, had a brainstorm as a kick from deep in his own half came past him and he grabbed it about 40 metres offside. That gave us the chance to work our way forward to the scrum from which Richard Hill kicked into the box — one of the classic scrum-half kicks — and Nigel and Will caught Jean-Baptiste Lafond as he made the catch and Will just took the ball off him and was driven over by the forwards. As he was walking back to halfway Mike Teague uttered the immortal words 'Finish 'em off, Webbie' and he did just that, drilling over the conversion and concluding a 19–10 victory.

The relief was enormous. We returned to the changing room and so missed the immediate sequel to the match, when Daniel Dubroca launched a violent verbal assault on David Bishop in the tunnel. The rumours came flitting through quite quickly but we saw nothing and, to be honest, we were so wrapped up in the result that all we could feel was the elation of the moment. Like the rest of the world we read about it in the papers the next day, by which time we were on our way to Scotland for the semi-final and a whole week of build-up and re-runs of 1990.

We had a day off on the Monday, when we golfed, but then it was back to training. Not only that, we had every opportunity to feel the tension growing because we were based in the heart of Edinburgh and everywhere you went you could hear the comments, see the newspaper hoardings: 'Sorry you'll be off home on Sunday', that sort of thing, all good-natured but it still puts you on edge. One afternoon Will and I were followed around by a group of local youngsters making snide comments, but you grin and bear it — and try to make sure the result doesn't go their way. Curiously, though, there wasn't the same fervour as before the grand-slam match of 1990; it was as though the Scots did not have the same conviction that they could win and, on the pitch just before the match when the anthems were played, 'Flower of Scotland' didn't have the same ring about it. Maybe they had looked at our game with France and thought, 'This time England are playing it for real.'

It was my 50th appearance for England – the first time any Englishman had reached that mark. A couple of nights beforehand Will asked if I would like to lead out the team to celebrate the occasion and that was a tremendous honour – though not quite the same as doing it at Twickenham since all you hear running out at Murrayfield is boos from the crowd who are waiting for their own heroes. They were keeping back a special cheer for John Jeffrey, who was leading out Scotland on his last home appearance before retiring from international rugby.

Nor was there any lack of resolve from JJ and the Scottish forwards. They kept their side in the game and we were unable to dominate up front as much as we hoped and it became a very tight game, notable only for kicks. Perhaps our best chance of a try was when I managed to get away down the left from Rob's break and as the cover converged I tried to get a pass away to Brian Moore inside me. On reflection, and particularly after seeing the video, I think I should have gone in low for the corner and if I hadn't known Brian was there I probably would have done. As it was, Finlay Calder got his hand to it but even so, it set up the position from which Rob dropped the goal that won the match. Neither team had been able to get away from the other: Gavin Hastings kicked two penalties to give Scotland the lead, Webbie kicked two for us on what was not his best day with the boot, but I think it was critical for Scotland that Gavin missed a straightforward penalty from 20 metres. That would have given them a 9–6 lead and although there were still 17 minutes left it would have given them a lead to defend; it was a definite let-off for us, although I believe we would have had the capacity to come back from it. As it was, Rob's goal was the clincher and, even if the style was disappointing, in the semi-final of the World Cup you win by whatever means come to hand. One point is enough.

To be frank my first feeling was almost of disbelief. Australia were anticipating a place in the final, New Zealand too, but for England, who were useless in 1987 and had promised so much in the last three years, it was unbelievable. You go into any competition wanting to win it but when you actually arrive at the position where you *can* win it, it's a tremendous achievement; you have proved so much, not only to yourselves but to your supporters and to the sceptics who didn't believe you could do it.

During the week that followed we knew what to expect from our opponents in the final – Australia, who had beaten New Zealand in the other semi-final in Dublin. After all, it was only four months since we had last played them, and even though they had thrashed us we had opened them up in the backs and we felt we could do the same again – and we didn't think we could dominate up front. Hence the much-debated change in our tactical approach at Twickenham on 2 November. People look back at that final now and remember England running the ball from everywhere, yet little of it went down the line; we ran through a variety of midfield moves but we never found the gaps in defence we expected, which speaks volumes for the tactical awareness of the Australians.

Their tackling was so sure and they always fed in another man to support the tackler and then fanned out in defence rather than committing more bodies to the ruck. Perhaps we could have kicked more than we did; perhaps our finishing was still not as sharp as it has to be if you are going to win World Cup finals. But the Australians made their way into a 9–0 lead through Michael Lynagh's first penalty and a converted try by Tony Daly and then defended their lead with considerable courage and skill. Webbie got three points back with a penalty, Lynagh kicked another goal, Rob put a dropped goal wide and Webbie's second penalty made it 12–6. We dominated the ball but we couldn't score the points. One of the main talking points afterwards was whether I would have scored from the move where Winters appeared in the line but David Campese knocked down his pass to me, conceding the penalty which was kicked. I can't honestly say that there was a case for a penalty try. I knew I was outside Campo but it was a long way from the line and I couldn't see who was in front of me. I felt I was in with a chance at the time but as I was looking inside to Winters, it was impossible to tell how the Australian cover lay; even watching on television afterwards the camera angles don't pick up where the defenders were coming from. Campo did what he normally does in such situations; he goes for the player and as he sees the pass coming, tries to smother everything, including the ball – which is how he scored against us at Twickenham in 1988.

Australia were world champions and, in retrospect, most people in the England side would admit that over the whole tournament they were the best side and deserved to win. But on the day we could have won, with a slight shift in our tactical approach; one of the points Geoff made afterwards was that Marty Roebuck, the Australian full-back, caught a high ball and took a hard tackle and was quite groggy – but we never kicked another ball to him. What made us as sore as anything was that we had heard so much during the tournament from the Australians – especially Campo – about how to play the game, but when it came to the final they shut up shop.

They appear to have a theory about playing a game to order, about creating a running game – which suits their conditions as well as their needs. But in the last few years England have offered a variety of styles, suitable to different occasions, without finding the ability to adapt during any given game itself. In 1990 we played an expansive game; in 1991 we closed it up; while in 1992 we returned to a more expansive game. In the World Cup we played in different ways during the tournament, and in the French game we were at our most clinical. But anyone watching us train during the World Cup would have seen us kicking very little; we trained with the ball in the hands but when it came to the final critics suggested that we could not switch to an open game without having adopted that style on a regular basis. Yet it was what we had prepared to do. On the day we gave it 100 per cent and came very close to winning. We had every reason to be proud.

13

Back to back

After the effort required for the World Cup the players could be forgiven for wondering whether there was life after the tournament. But how often is it the case that the players look forward while the supporters still look back? For some, returning to club rugby was relaxation while for Roger Uttley, England's coach, it was time to bow out gracefully and return to the normality of life on the school staff at Harrow. His position went to Richard Best, who in the course of seventeen years had played for, captained and coached Harlequins, the club which now provided nearly half the England XV.

The players put away the gold medals they received from the Queen after the World Cup final was over – Australia, the winners, received platinum medals – and went back to business, to the daily routine of job and family and, in their sport, of league rugby. Jerry Guscott said 'no' once more to rugby league offers, Brian Moore sat down with International Board representatives to explain what exactly the players hoped for in commercial terms from their rugby fame, and the Board itself decided that the game might be more exciting if they encouraged more try-scoring by making the try worth five points – a recommendation which was approved at the subsequent annual meeting.

Rob Andrew, England's fly-half, moved jobs to work in Toulouse. Mike Teague, suffering damage to both shoulders and an ankle after playing, he said, one game too many, could not work and looked for compensation for his injuries from the Rugby Football Union – player and union duly reached an agreement. Paul Ackford, England lock, police inspector, newspaper columnist, retired, though he was tempted back by Harlequins, his club, for the Pilkington Cup final five months later. David Campese, the bête noire of the England team and ever unpredictable, decided that perhaps he would not retire from international rugby after all. South Africa formed a new governing body and was warmly welcomed back into international sport in the *spring of 1992. And Rory and Wendy Underwood looked forward to an extension to their family, their second daughter, Alexandra, duly appearing in December.*

Five and a half weeks of intense concentration, playing, training media, functions, ended with the William Webb Ellis Trophy – 'Bill' as the Australians call it – returning to the southern hemisphere and on the Monday I was back at work. I think Wendy would not have minded a couple of days together but the boys at the squadron were very good, there were no great post mortems, and it was something of a relief to get away from the rugby. I missed two weekends with Leicester; I didn't train, I just went home and rested and returned to the normal domestic routine.

I returned to training one Monday evening, in the week Leicester were to play Wasps. It was drizzling and I seriously considered not going; I don't recall consciously thinking about retirement but I felt I could do without it. I was tired, it was wet, I could have been home with the family. However, I turned up for the session, which was held on the Recreation Ground in front of the jail, across the road from Leicester's ground – it was not the most wonderful training night and I mentioned to Tony Russ, the club's director of coaching, that I didn't think the attitude was all it might be. He suggested that I might be noticing the difference between five weeks with England and the standard of first-division club rugby, which was a fair point, but I came away with my level of enthusiasm at an all-time low. The Thursday training, on the main Welford Road pitch, went better but it was not until I got into the game against Wasps that my own attitude perked up.

The sense of deflation was inevitable I suppose. And while England had been reaching such an emotional climax, club rugby in the country as a whole had been very flat. Everyone had focused on the World Cup and no one except the faithful few was paying any attention to the club programme. In addition Leicester had been through a difficult two months; they had toured successfully in Canada pre-season but all the good work they had done disappeared when divisional and county calls meant they played with a different team each week. Morale was not high, particularly after being well beaten at Gloucester in the first league game of the season, so everyone revived after the win over Wasps and it helped me rediscover my own enthusiasm.

The question that was being asked, though, was how many members of the World Cup squad would retire. As it happened we lost only one, Paul Ackford, who announced his retirement three weeks after the final; I was surprised because my view was that mid-season was not the time to go. With the championship coming up it seemed a waste of so much work, but Paul made his own decision – to go before he was pushed, though that didn't seem likely at the time – and I was already clear in my own mind that this would be my last season of international rugby. None the less all of us were as fit as we had ever been and it seemed right to go through the whole season before calling it a day. Most of the older squad members gave themselves some time for reflection, which allowed a period of recovery from the sense of anti-climax which followed the tournament.

Everyone was notified of my intentions, on both the RAF and the rugby sides, and with the air cleared I could happily prepare both for the club's programme and for the 1992 Five Nations. The first training session for which England gathered felt really good, all the buzz and the banter going on, and in one evening we were back into the swing of things. The attitude had not changed for anyone, even though we had won the 1991 grand slam and reached the World Cup final: another season, another championship, another set of hurdles to be overcome. Scotland away for starters is not, and has never been, easy. It is a measure, too, of the esteem felt by the players for the Five Nations competition. The World Cup is every four years – some people's international careers may start and finish within that time span – and though it now means that there is a gradual build-up to each World Cup, our own international rugby means as much as a Bledisloe Cup match does to an Australian or a New Zealander.

While we had lost Ackers, Scotland had lost Finlay Calder and John Jeffrey through retirement and, through injury, Gary Armstrong, their scrum-half. England regard Gary as one of Scotland's primary play-makers and a man we need to control – just as we felt obliged to make plans to stop Pierre Berbizier when he was France's scrum-half. Gary played wonderfully well behind a struggling pack at Twickenham in 1991 and he needs to be bottled up. We also needed to integrate our own newcomers to the pack, Martin Bayfield and Tim Rodber, and welcome back Dewi Morris – and what a championship he had.

Dewi's selection at scrum-half was a bit of a surprise but none the less understandable. Richard Hill is an exceptional player and his pass ranks with the fastest but he had lost a lot of speed – perhaps through too much long-distance training which has dulled that sharp edge he used to have when he broke. The argument that Dewi might pose a greater threat round the fringes was not a factor; Hillie was obeying instructions during the World Cup, that either the forwards used the ball or it was out to Rob. It's never easy to know the right time to change but on this occasion it worked and it earned Dewi reward for faithful service on the replacements' bench during the autumn. Both he and David Pears were great ambassadors even when they knew they were not going to play unless we suffered injury.

We had another important new face in the shape of Dick Best, who had taken over from Roger Uttley as coach after the World Cup. That brought a new way of thinking to the squad. Roger's virtues had a lot to do with his own experience of what happens on the field, in getting players motivated, in organising the forwards. He had little to do with the backs, where the tactical approach broadly devolved on Geoff Cooke, but with Dick's introduction Geoff found his workload reduced because Dick, even though he was a forward himself, can think as a back too. Dick had been on tour with us in Australia and Fiji the previous summer without being used to a great extent but most of us knew him and the players from Harlequins, his own club, were used to his ways. He introduced a new element to training, which was good, and I think he probably toned down the approach he used with Harlequins and with London – which, from what I hear, was a bit like a sergeant-major or a school teacher, which is how Roger came across sometimes.

Dick did very well. He was conscious of the position he had found himself in on tour, when he was given a lot of stick because he had to act as baggage-master for much of the time, but he's his own man, a demanding coach with his own style. He was diplomatic enough to bring out any positive thoughts the players had to offer and helped, along with Geoff and Will, to create an atmosphere which brought the best out of backs and forwards – which was not far away in any case.

Even so, in his first match in charge, it took us a while to settle at Murrayfield. The line-out didn't go to plan at all and their loose play had lost none of its enthusiasm; it's strange the effect a Scottish shirt has, even on an Englishman like Ian Smith, Gloucester's flanker! We edged our way into a 6–3 lead before I got away for that try which had been so long coming against Scotland. It came about because Gavin Hastings had been so intimately involved in the whole game and when he came on a short pass he was hit by Tim Rodber and Peter Winterbottom so that the ball squirted loose to Rob and he popped it up to Simon Halliday. Out it went to Jerry and the ball came to me in space – more space than you ever see in an international because Tony Stanger, my opposite number, had got tied up in the previous action. I even had time to think about how to beat Craig Chalmers who was covering across; Craig's not slow and I pondered whether to straighten him up before deciding that, with so much space to run into, I might just as well take off towards the touchline. Craig went for the tap-tackle but he was too far away and I enjoyed my long run in.

That was encouragement for everyone in a game where we struggled for possession in the first half, but we were not allowed to sit back and enjoy it. Andy Nicol, Scotland's scrum-half, made a break and Gavin nearly squeezed into the corner. They were given a five-metre scrum and timed their shove to perfection; another referee might have said the ball came in early but as far as I could see it was all in the timing. While our forwards were looking to settle into the scrum the Scots went down, the ball went in and we were going back so fast that Derek White had an easy job touching down. Still Webbie kicked a couple of goals, and midway through the second half Tim went off after a bang on the head and Dean replaced him – which must have been a daunting sight for the Scots. It certainly tightened up the loose ball and it was Dean who laid on the pass from which Jerry dropped his first international goal. I was standing beside him at the time and thought, 'No, he isn't – he is' and it was a beautiful effort, straight between the posts. I remember standing alongside Hugo Porta on the halfway line at Sydney when the World XV played Australia in 1988 and had the same feeling of disbelief when he lined up a dropped goal and scored it with no evidence of power, merely a sweet swing of the boot. Jerry's was almost as impressive and after that we started making inroads: Simon meandered into midfield and Dewi, indefatigable as ever, pitched up for the try.

It was a good result, 25–7, while leaving us plenty to work on, notably at the set pieces. But this time we had the benefit of going straight through our programme with no breaks, four games in seven weeks and no loss of momentum. On the surface the fixture with Ireland, at Twickenham, looked easy because they had just lost at home to Wales; but they had run Australia close in their World Cup quarter-final and we have learned from bitter experience to take absolutely nothing for granted. Still, we didn't expect to be six points up before the match was a minute old; we had been working on kick-offs because we were not very good at recovering ball kicked around the opposing ten-metre line and the long kick-off is usually marked and returned to touch or touched down in-goal (though the new law will change that). As a wing you can run 50 yards and end up just short, but here we were looking at landing the ball just outside the Irish

22 and Webbie has such good control of his kicking that we could rely on him doing so. He has worked exceptionally hard on that part of his game; when he started his career he used to worry about every aspect of his game whereas now he is far more relaxed about his general game and works at Bath with their specialist kicking coach. He does that for an hour each Sunday and the dividends, in his goal-kicking and his line-kicking, have been obvious.

At Twickenham the kick-off descended on Phil Matthews, who was tackled at the same time; the ball went loose, Rob pounced on it to set up the ruck, Jerry went short and established a maul, the ball popped out and Webbie went for the gap to score a try in something like 23 seconds. The Irish returned with interest, Ralph Keyes running over unopposed as our drift defence drifted too wide when Rob was wrapped up in a maul, but by half-time we were 24–9 up and never going to be caught. Dewi had scored after a great run down the left with support from Brian Moore, and Jerry added another just to prove that we could score other than by a pushover from a five-metre scrum. Dick Best had managed to persuade the forwards to let the backs have the ball from close-range scrums and Brian, the pack leader, reluctantly agreed. The move is based on the score Will made against France in 1989, when there is a miss-pass in the centre and the wing comes on the scissors; on this occasion I came in short, checked Brendan Mullin, and Jerry went round on the outside to score. The second half gave us a chance to elaborate: I scored in the corner from a planned move, helped by Webbie, Hallers rolled his way over and Webbie finished off after Will had surged through and laid back the ball for Jerry. It was a good game for Webbie, who finished with 22 points on his way to a record championship tally.

So, for the second time in four months, we returned to the Parc des Princes. Since our last visit the French had been in turmoil; quite apart from the immediate aftermath to the Dubroca scandal which brought about his resignation, Jean Trillo, their assistant coach, had retired, so had Serge Blanco, and they had had a presidential election, ending the reign of Albert Ferrasse after 23 years. There was a new regime in charge, a new coach in Pierre Berbizier, and new players, several from the Bègles-Bordeaux club which had won the French championship in 1991 based on the strength of their forwards. The whole French scene had been shaken up after the World Cup and was still settling into place, and their new-look team had yet to establish itself on the international scene.

One other consequence of the World Cup match was the resurrection of the French conspiracy theory, that the Anglo-Saxon world, in the shape of referees, is against them. After the World Cup quarter-final Blanco had said that he felt David Bishop had ignored English foul play, and one or two items in English newspapers stirred up more bad blood. Mooro did not help a great deal by saying that he always expected dirty play when he encountered the French – that's why we call him the 'pit bull' because every now and again he savages someone or something. But I believe the French have to live with the consequences of selecting the side they did to play against us; they may have taken exception to some of the stories printed in England about French rugby but they should have used them, as the other home countries would have done, to stiffen their resolve rather than to get even. I think some of their players went out against us not fully in control of themselves – lights on but no one at home, as it were.

I went into the game quite confident, knowing we could win again – as we had in our previous four meetings. I expected a hard game and, in the first half, we got it because they played really well and were 4–3 up with only two minutes left before half-time. Moreover we had lost Rob with an eye injury and David Pears came on for his first championship game – and started walking towards the French side, he was so disorientated as he came on to the pitch. It was a big moment for him but he took his chance really well, all credit to him, and he had settled down by the time we attacked the right-hand side of the field just before the interval. Winters set up the position for a five-metre scrum which creaked and groaned and lurched sideways before the French collapsed and Stephen Hilditch, the referee, awarded England a penalty try. I was on the far side of the field so it was hard to see who was at fault; it's one of those situations where, if the decision goes against you, you feel hard done by and if it goes for you, you feel very happy.

Whether it was that which led to the French downfall I don't know, but their discomfort was compounded by Webbie's try and suddenly they trailed 15–4. Jerry helped make it by getting outside Philippe Sella and making as though to chip. Webbie came into the line beautifully and I thought, 'Here we go, two to one' because I was outside my marker in support, but suddenly Lafond drifted on to me and the way was open for Webbie. The television shows Sella prepared to cover across on me thinking that Lafond would take the man with the ball, except to his horror he found Lafond going in the same direction and Webbie was in unopposed. In the second half the French went to pieces; Sella, their captain, had been suffering from dulled hearing after a painful knock on the head early on and it forced him off. Nothing they did could find a way through our defence and, to cap it all, there was a clattering collision between two of their backs and Jean-Luc Sadourny, Sella's replacement, went off with blood streaming from his face. In the confusion Pearsie collected the ball, Winters and Mooro provided the link and I was over near the posts. That was the final straw. The French half was like a casualty ward; Christophe Mougeot hurt a leg trying to tackle me and went off, Fabien Galthié had taken over as captain and was clearly not in control, and with ten minutes left Grégoire Lascubé joined the queue leaving the field after being sent off. He could be seen quite clearly at the back of a ruck kicking Martin Bayfield's head with his studs and the touch judge had no choice but to recommend that Lascubé go. Jean-François Tordo, the flanker, was lucky not to join him because he came flying into a ruck a couple of minutes later, nowhere near the ball, but in fact it was Vincent Moscato, the hooker, who was also dismissed for butting in a scrum.

It was such a shame, for the French, for the game. For an hour they had caused us all sorts of problems and Laurent Cabannes, their open-side flanker, was one of the best players on the field. But it has always been the case that, if events are not going in their favour, they start talking among themselves and become disjointed. This was a young, inexperienced side but you have to wonder at the attitude of some of the forwards Berbizier picked. At the dinner afterwards there was talk about the difference in interpretation of the laws and Stephen Hilditch was invited to referee in France (which he later did) but, for doing what they did, the two forwards deserved to be sent off. Sadly there was no contact between the players in the big banqueting hall; we were at one end, the French at the other and the twain did not meet.

So we were left with three out of three and the first back-to-back grand slam for 68 years staring us in the face. A formality against the Welsh? Not exactly. Of course we were favourites but Wales had restored some of the pride lost over the previous three years and we were all wary of the dormant dragon. But if there was any fire it was doused by another quick Twickenham try, within two minutes of the start; Will climbed high after Rob's kick and fell over the line for the score and thereafter it was only resolute Welsh defence that prevented England really going to town. In that respect Wales played well and made us work for everything, but they offered no threat in attack. At least they stopped me and Dewi scoring a try and completing a set for the championship, which we would both have prized. I had a glimmer of two chances. One was when Rob chipped through and Ieuan Evans and I competed for the touch but the ball was always bouncing away from me. The other was when I got outside Ieuan and had only Mike Rayer, the replacement full-back, ahead but I was on an outside curve and couldn't change direction; looking back I should have chipped but I opted for the body check and he was able to force me into touch. I expect if I had chipped, Jerry, who was sneaking around inside me, would have got up for the try!

That was a disappointment but 24–0 was a good, solid performance, if not the spectacle we would all have enjoyed. Partly for that reason the elation of the achievement did not match that of a year earlier. Against France in 1991 the result was in doubt until the final whistle, whereas against the Welsh there was never any prospect that we would lose. And, of course, second time around can never match the first. The difference, though, was that I knew it was my last game for England. Some of the papers had carried the story on the morning of the match but I had no idea how many of the crowd who swarmed on to the pitch knew and I had vaguely hoped to go out on the balcony in front of the committee box in the West Stand to wave goodbye. As it turned out, though, we all went up the steps to wave to the crowd who stood and cheered and sang for the team.

It was an emotional moment for me. I wanted to say goodbye, and thank you, and, perhaps, selfishly, I wanted the moment to myself. But in the end it was appropriate enough that the whole team should have been there, because we had shared so much and there were others too who would not be playing for England again. At the time of writing there have been no firm decisions but it seems possible that, for big Wade, for Hallers and for Skins, the sands have run out. There was a very big lump in my throat as I did my first radio interview. I know some of the boys still think I might be back, but I knew it was time to go.

14

Try and try again

Few of those fortunate enough to have watched Gerald Davies playing on the wing for Wales and the British Lions in the 1970s did not treasure the moments. He played 46 times for his country and scored 20 tries, at a time when there were few easy matches; chances, when they arose, had to be taken. Davies is also one of the few players in modern times who could translate his talents from the playing field to the written word, which he does with great facility for The Times *and in the various books to which he has contributed. No one knows better the art of wing play and his assessment of Rory Underwood, who was still at Barnard Castle School when Davies ended his international playing career in 1978, could not be bettered.*

'*A wing needs pace more than any other player in the three-quarter line. Rory Underwood has it in abundance. This is his outstanding quality and has made him a great finisher; he stands alongside Patrice Lagisquet of France and Ian Williams of Australia (though we did not see enough of him) as the wingers of the era with genuine pace. Ieuan Evans of Wales has the same quality but never played in a consistently good team in which he could flourish. Given half a yard you could not imagine anyone catching that quartet.*

It takes all sorts. John Kirwan had power. Others, not so well-equipped physically, need to be clever, the game running instinctively in their blood and having their wits as constant companions. At the risk of shredding a monumental career, let us say that David Campese does not have real pace, not genuine run-like-the-wind speed. He succeeds, instead, because of the infinite variety of his other skills, a player possessed of a mind who controls what the rest of his body should do in the complexities of a game. For all his tricks, he knows what he is up to.

Because of the intricate nature of his style – the veering in and out, the change of mood and direction – Campese, like the great illusionist he is, only gives the impression of speed. Angles, not straight lines, are his preferred route, connivance the method. He is a ball-player. He would be bored if he did not have anyone to bamboozle.

Rory Underwood is not of Campese's kind. He did not have to be. The essence of Underwood is that he is a sprinter, a man of the track. He has a sprinter's physique, broad of shoulder, thick of thigh. He has a sprinter's style, a high knee lift and, if he did not have to carry a ball, an arm action held close to his sides and which seemed to propel him forward. Athletes are fast on the track. But they cannot transfer it to the football pitch. Underwood could, and did, like JJ Williams of Wales before him.

There is an economy of movement in Underwood's running. Good running form matters. There is no panic under stress. Witness the long run for his try against Scotland at Murrayfield in 1992, or the equally long run against Australia on tour in 1988 – eyes always looking forward, the brief sideways glance which did not deflect his search for the try-line, the tape at the finishing line of the athlete's race. Usually, in rugby players who know little of athletics training, heads begin to roll and the shoulder to stiffen as the strain of a long sprint begins to tell. Underwood maintained an athlete's style.

Latterly he became confident too, in the challenge of direct body contact. He dipped his shoulder into opponents. This must have arisen because of the quality of England's preparation: solid muscle from weight training encourages the sense of well-being, of hardness and toughness to take on all comers. He became adept at taking the half-chances close to the line: the try, for instance, from a short-range tapped penalty against Ireland in 1992.

He sniffed the line, knew where it was and, preferring the direct route, knew how to get there. This was his great strength. He could pause momentarily, check the cover defence, and move away again. It was elegantly done. At no time was this better demonstrated than in Leicester's 28–18 victory at Northampton in 1990.

He scored three tries that day, an overcast afternoon, a wet pitch. The first came when he was given half a gap. He went beyond the initial line of defence and then, without any perceptible loss of pace, he leaned slightly to the inside and, having forced the full back to hesitate, steered a course on the outside and scored in the corner. The second try was a long sprint but he had to beat a whole host of players converging in cover defence. He, the sprinter, made them all look like middle-distance runners. It was a majestic performance. He simply skimmed over the greasy surface.

There was such clarity of intention and execution, which distinguishes the great performer from the merely good. He swerved with the best but had no sidestep. Speed off the mark over a short distance took him away from the tackler. Half a gap was usually all he needed. He left the observer, this one at any rate, with the impression that his feet did not touch the ground as he ran; he glided, which befits a Flight

*Lieutenant I suppose. The photograph, which almost every newspaper
seemed to use, of his 1992 Murrayfield try captures perfectly the essence
of Underwood.'*

During the last ten years I have been fortunate enough to play against
some of the great wings in world rugby but the players I remember best
are those with whom I have played, rather than those I have played
against. It is a product of being part of an England squad which has
stayed together for so long, though it is only fair to add that, while he
was not part of the team which has played so well between 1989 and
1992, Mickey Harrison will remain one of my favourites – since he
was the best man at my wedding he has to be!

I played with Mickey for Yorkshire and the North, as well as for
England, and it was at that lower level that we really enjoyed
ourselves. England did not see the best of Mickey; he won 15 caps and
scored seven tries, which is a pretty good strike rate, but all of them
came overseas – two interceptions in his first two internationals, in
New Zealand (I wouldn't have minded a couple against the All
Blacks), and five during the 1987 World Cup. During his time in the
Five Nations championship England were a very inhibited team and
the best he could manage was to force a penalty try against the Scots in
1987.

But playing for the county and the division was very different. It was
the kind of rugby I most enjoy, where we could all express ourselves,
and Mickey and I were given full scope in back divisions controlled by
such good players as Alan Old and Rob Andrew. We had licence to
run, from anywhere, and you would often find Mickey turning up to
support on my side of the field, and vice versa. Even now that his
England days are over Mickey has gone on serving Wakefield, as try-
scorer and captain – both of us will have fond memories with which to
bore our children when we are older.

But the best of those I have played against, in no particular order,
must be David Campese, John Kirwan and Patrice Lagisquet. They
offer a diversity of gifts which helped make them players of the highest
quality. Campo, Australia's most-capped player and the world's
leading try-scorer with 48 (at the time of writing), has an unfortunate
habit of offering advice about the playing of the game to all and sundry
whether they want it or not, but as a player pure and simple he is
completely unpredictable, which is part of the fascination. He's not
outstandingly fast, nor is he the world's best defender, but he has
exceptional ball skills allied to a smart brain. He has a vision for the

game matched by very few, which permits him to identify opportunities before anyone else and he has the nerve to go for those
opportunities; he isn't worried, either, if what he tries doesn't come
off. He's always said that he's out there to entertain and he lives up to
that. He has a big sidestep, very good hands and he can kick the ball a
long, long way which is part of the reason why he's played so many
games at full-back.

Kirwan, the New Zealander, is a different kettle of fish altogether
although both he and Campo have taken to playing their rugby in Italy
of late. Kirwan is much the bigger man – 6 ft 3 in as opposed to 5 ft 10
in and well over a stone heavier at 14 st 7 lb – and for a man his size he
is fast, though not outstandingly quick. The power, the sheer physique
of his play has added a dimension to New Zealand rugby over the last
eight years and he has a hand-off you would not want to get in the way
of. His qualities were seen to tremendous effect when he scored against
the Italians in the opening game of the 1987 World Cup – the defence
was not of the highest quality but none the less he had to run 80 yards,
dummying, changing pace and direction until he had reached the line
for a tremendous try which, quite rightly, brought the house down.

Lagisquet, the Frenchman whose last international season was sadly
marred by injury, was the fastest of the three. Now he was quick.
Quicker than me? Hard to say because unless you find yourself in a
straight one-on-one contest, you never know for sure. Kirwan was
easy to defend against because you would show him the outside and
then cut him down; Campo was harder to mark because of his
unpredictability but I would show him the outside and he would never
take it so I had to be prepared to check or rely on the cover if he elected
to cut inside. But Lagisquet had an enormous sidestep and I found the
greatest difficulty defending against him; I always felt I had to rely on
other backs covering across in the drift defence to take him if he chose
to go inside me and even if he took the outside he had a good body
swerve which leaned him away from the defender.

You come to know, with experience, which way most players will
go. Ieuan Evans, Wales's captain during the 1991 World Cup and a
colleague on the 1989 British Lions tour, is not the quickest but he has
a good sidestep so I would always try to offer him space on the outside.
I would not risk offering the same room to Lagisquet, who was not
nicknamed the 'Bayonne Express' for nothing.

As far as my own play on the wing is concerned I never consciously
modelled myself on any players. I received the best advice on how to
beat a man very early in my career from Glenn Robertson, who played

his club rugby on the wing for Northampton and coached the England colts – as well as lending a hand, later on, to preparing the London divisional side. Glenn watched me playing for Durham colts against Yorkshire colts, when I was put away twice but couldn't quite beat my marker, and he gave me a couple of tips which have stood the test of time. The first was to do with change of pace: slowing so as to draw a defender towards you and then accelerating away, which has become one of my most effective weapons. The second was how to beat a cover tackler by cutting back inside with a change of direction.

The main criticism throughout my career was that I failed to concentrate for the full 80 minutes – which is the perennial winger's problem. On the fringe of the game for much of the time it's easy enough to drift, mentally, and suddenly find that when one isolated chance comes your way you spill it. In some ways, knowing the lack of physical involvement, it's one of the hardest positions in which to play but it was not a criticism I readily accepted because I was never conscious of it myself. In mid-career, indeed, the entire England team was seldom error-free and you had to work hard to make sure the unexpected did not happen; nowadays the team is much more together as a unit, the pieces fit together far better. But at no time was I aware of an absence of concentration.

I wish now that I had practised kicking out of hand from a far earlier age. I was so frequently able to rely on my speed to get me out of trouble that I did not pay enough attention to kicking, at a time when both wings have become also supplementary full-backs and have to possess some of the full-back's skills. I could usually be relied upon to find touch out of defence but not the sort of touch that would cause a weary forward to turn round and give me the thumbs-up for not forcing him to trudge back into his own 22 and defend grimly. If I had been able to chip-kick better, too, I might have scored in my last international, against Wales.

Nor was it until comparatively late in my career that I really started to work on passing off my left hand, the weaker hand. I am pretty confident about hitting the target, the support player, but I can't spin-pass off my left. These are the kind of skills that any aspiring wing needs to master because rugby is a game of continuity; if you want to be a good wing, you need basic speed obviously, but also an awareness of support and how to use it.

You also need a fair degree of courage because international rugby is now even more physical a game than it used to be; there are big, fast men making very big tackles. Although that has not been a problem in my senior career I'm sure I have been bolstered by the people with whom I've played. If you stay long enough in a side and develop friendships with your colleagues, you know that when you are on the field together you are not going to let them down. You see players like Peter Winterbottom and Mike Teague making tackle after tackle, far more in one game than you are required, as a wing, to make, and you know that when your turn comes you must show yourself their equal.

I suppose if I have been able to leave any kind of imprint on the game it is for my dive to score, one-handed, at the corner-flag. It's not hard to do but you have to be certain in your own mind about selling yourself completely to make sure of the try; you have to know the right time to start your dive at the corner and forget about the defence coming hell-for-leather across to push you out, and if you go in low enough, it's very difficult to stop. A bit like an aeroplane coming in to land, I suppose. Some wings may worry about exposing their bodies completely to the tackle, by stretching out for the try-line, but I have never been hurt scoring a try.

In fact it's much the same as stretching for the line in the middle of the park but, for some reason, players going into the corner tend not to do so and far too many either try to cut back inside – and get caught – or look for the support and hurl the ball infield rather than launch themselves for the corner. Again, as in so many aspects of play, you commit yourself – to the tackle, to falling on the loose ball, to making the catch. If you are tentative, or frightened of being injured, you will not succeed.

It's worth emphasising, too, how much sheer enjoyment I have derived from playing rugby – and that is the main reason for being involved for so long. Very few players set out with the specific intention of representing their country – that is how their careers happen to develop. If you play the game to enjoy it, then opportunities occur through that enjoyment because the better you play the greater the pleasure. Winning is part of the enjoyment too and, happily, England have had their share of that now.

Of the tries I have scored, several stand out – not all of them for England although I think that my first international try, against France in Paris in 1984, will stick in the memory. It was, after all, the first of the 35 and there is never anything like the first time. Mind, my first try at Twickenham was enjoyable because in four years of international rugby – 22 games – I had managed only four tries and none of them at home. That was against Ireland in 1988 and the feeling was not so much of pure pleasure as unadulterated relief!

Geoff Cooke remembers a try I scored for Yorkshire, long before anyone outside the North had taken much notice of me, and I have a certain fondness for one that came for Leicester against London Welsh, which must have covered about 70 metres. In fact when Leicester's backs were at their height we scored some tremendous tries, too many to recollect accurately; even when most of Leicester's international backs had retired we were still capable of conjuring some magic, like in 1991 when Brian Smith, the Australian who played for Ireland and later went to rugby league, was still playing fly-half for the club. Against Liverpool St Helens Peter Buckton, an old friend from Yorkshire days, was tearing across the field wreaking havoc, so from one line-out I told Brian to take the ball forward himself before popping it inside to me. He did so, Bucko shot across, their No 8 was slow getting out and I went straight through, changed direction to beat the scrum-half and was able to beat the wing for pace to score after a good 60 or 70 yards. Brian quite enjoyed it too!

I suppose the most important try was the one, again against Ireland, in Dublin in 1991. It was the third leg of the grand slam and we were losing 7–6 with the Irish forwards fighting a magnificent rearguard action. There were only eight minutes left on the clock when Jerry Guscott was checked in midfield but Dean Richards took it on and Simon Hodgkinson was able to clear it left to me on a scissors. There was still quite a lot of work to do with 30 yards to go and a lot of defenders around, but I managed to slip three of them and run in for the score which made sure that we won because at that stage of the game they were not winning enough of the ball to have any chance of a comeback. That was very satisfying, although Brian Smith may have been less impressed on that occasion – he was on the losing side.

There are several people, too, with whom I have always enjoyed playing. Inevitably they are backs, so apologies to all the 'donkeys' who have made it possible by actually winning the ball for the back division to use in the first place. Clive Woodward, at Leicester, I have already mentioned as the most outstanding support player in my experience and Les Cusworth, in the same side, was a wonderful tactician and, moreover, brought enormous fun to the game – although he was as competitive as the next man.

The other two played half-back together for Yorkshire and England less frequently than they might have done. That was because Nigel Melville, who first began to attract attention as an 18-year-old back in 1979, suffered such an appalling string of injuries. Nigel was a wonderful passer of the ball from scrum-half; he possessed the quickest pair of hands I have seen, he had lots of pace and that he had courage is illustrated by the number of times he came back from his injuries.

Courage is one of the virtues that Rob Andrew possesses too, though perhaps he required a different sort to Nigel. Having played with Rob at school, and at every one of the higher representative levels, I suppose I can appreciate him as well as anyone and no one could have been more pleased that he finally achieved the international recognition that has been his for the last three years. My admiration for the way he has emerged from the criticism he received during his playing career is total, and since he looks set to go on playing international rugby for a few more seasons, it does look as though the record of England appearances – he has 48 to my 55 – will pass from one Barnard Castle boy to another.

The last word

By Rob Andrew, England fly-half 1985–

Forty-one tries in 15 matches. Not a bad record. No, not the record Rory holds for England – not that I'm a great one for records and he certainly isn't – but it's one that has always stuck in my mind when recalling our school days together. It was, in fact, our last school rugby term, September to December 1981.

If my memory serves me correctly we had been in the same school teams since 8 September 1974. Remarkably Rory was always on the left wing and I was always wearing the No 10 shirt. Many people have been kind enough to point out that it is amazing he has stayed in the game for 18 years with a fly-half who kicked the ball so much! However, his burning desire to run up and down a rugby field after the ball had been nurtured long before our England playing days.

Those 41 tries in 15 matches were really the beginning of Rory's future international career. He was always blessed with great speed throughout school but it was only during his last year that a considerable amount of power was added to his game – though through no great effort of his own because Rory was never the most enthusiastic of trainers, especially where the physical side of the game was concerned. But he suddenly developed this great natural athleticism, something most of us can merely dream about as we perspire in the gym. This was to become his greatest asset, remarked upon by Tom McNab when England's preparations occupied a higher plane after the 1987 World Cup. 'Rory is one of the finest untrained athletes I have ever worked with,' Tom said. High praise indeed.

From December 1981 to the present the path has gone ever upward to the world-class wing that Rory is recognised as today. Durham colts, England colts, Durham seniors and Yorkshire, the North, the RAF, Middlesbrough, Leicester, England, the Barbarians, the British Lions. It is an extraordinary list, with records tumbling along the way.

I have been very fortunate to travel to many parts of the world through rugby, and many of those trips have been in Rory's company.

During those long tours you come to know your playing colleagues very well indeed and I think three words sum up Rory's qualities – loyalty, honesty and calm. That latter quality – you might describe it as laid-back in today's parlance – will register with all who have had the pleasure of knowing Rory, however briefly. Little has changed; whether it is Les Cusworth or Dusty Hare recounting stories of his early days training with Leicester and England, or Nigel Melville and Huw Davies frequently finding him asleep on the floor of their flat in London, the same relaxed, friendly person remains.

Many of the situations, at home and overseas, in which Rory and I have been together have been highly charged but I have rarely seen him have a cross word with anyone (a rare feat indeed considering the England teams in which he has played), nor has anyone a bad word to say about Rory (save, perhaps, when he was last by a long way in a 3000m timed run back in 1986 – I think he thought it was a walking race!).

He has finished his international career with a personal reputation second to none and a playing record which needs no introduction. However, as far as the rugby is concerned, those who know Rory well will have seen a significant change in his contribution over the years, on and off the field. That change coincided with a differing attitude among many players during the course of Geoff Cooke's management, which has so obviously influenced England's success. Rory is one of the few players to have gone through so long an international career without being dropped, a remarkable achievement, but subtle pressures – such as switching him to the right wing – have had a marked effect. During his early days he was scarcely involved in what the team was attempting to do; by the end of his career he had strong views on the development of the team which, I believe, could be seen on the pitch.

We have been virtually members of the same teams for nearly 18 years – at Barnard Castle, at Middlesbrough, with Yorkshire, the North, England and the Lions – and it will be strange to be in a side without Rory Underwood lurking out on the left wing. But the memories remain, the memories of such wonderful tries in a golden period for English rugby. Isn't that what you always dreamed about?

Career record

RORY UNDERWOOD: Born Middlesbrough 19 June 1963
Height: 5 ft 9 in   Weight: 13 st 5 lb
Position: Left wing
Clubs: Middlesbrough, Leicester, Royal Air Force
Counties: Durham, Yorkshire
Division: North

International appearances for England (55)

Date	Opponents	Venue	Result	Tries	Position
1984					
18.2.84:	Ireland	Twickenham	won 12–9		11
3.3.84:	France	Paris	lost 18–32	1	11
17.3.84:	Wales	Twickenham	lost 15–24		11
3.11.84:	Australia	Twickenham	lost 3–19		11
1985					
5.1.85:	Romania	Twickenham	won 22–15		11
2.2.85:	France	Twickenham	drawn 9–9		11
16.3.85:	Scotland	Twickenham	won 10–7		11
30.3.85:	Ireland	Dublin	lost 10–13	1	11
20.4.85:	Wales	Cardiff	lost 15–24		11
1986					
18.1.86:	Wales	Twickenham	won 21–18		11
1.3.86:	Ireland	Twickenham	won 25–20		11
15.3.86:	France	Paris	lost 10–29		11
1987					
7.2.87:	Ireland	Dublin	lost 0–17		11
21.2.87:	France	Twickenham	lost 15–19		11
7.3.87:	Wales	Cardiff	lost 12–19		11
4.4.87:	Scotland	Twickenham	won 21–12		11
23.5.87:	Australia	Sydney	lost 6–19		11
30.5.87:	Japan	Sydney	won 60–7	2	11
8.6.87:	Wales	Brisbane	lost 3–16		11

1988

16.1.88: France	Paris	lost 9–10		11
6.2.88: Wales	Twickenham	lost 3–11		11
5.3.88: Scotland	Edinburgh	won 9–6		14
19.3.88: Ireland	Twickenham	won 35–3	2	14
23.4.88: Ireland	Dublin	won 21–10	1	11
29.5.88: Australia	Brisbane	lost 16–22	1	11
12.6.88: Australia	Sydney	lost 8–28	1	11
16.6.88: Fiji	Suva	won 25–12	2	11
5.11.88: Australia	Twickenham	won 28–19	2	11

1989

4.2.89: Scotland	Twickenham	drawn 12–12		14
18.2.89: Ireland	Dublin	won 16–3		14
4.3.89: France	Twickenham	won 11–0		14
18.3.89: Wales	Cardiff	lost 9–12		14
13.5.89: Romania	Bucharest	won 58–3		14
4.11.89: Fiji	Twickenham	won 58–23	5	14

1990

20.1.90: Ireland	Twickenham	won 23–0	1	14
3.2.90: France	Paris	won 26–7	1	14
17.2.90: Wales	Twickenham	won 34–6	2	11
17.3.90: Scotland	Edinburgh	lost 7–13		11
3.11.90: Argentina	Twickenham	won 51–0	3	11

1991

19.1.91: Wales	Cardiff	won 25–6		11
16.2.91: Scotland	Twickenham	won 21–12		11
2.3.91: Ireland	Dublin	won 16–7	1	11
16.3.91: France	Twickenham	won 21–19	1	11
20.7.91: Fiji	Suva	won 28–12	1	14
27.7.91: Australia	Sydney	lost 15–40		14
3.10.91: New Zealand	Twickenham	lost 12–18		14
8.10.91: Italy	Twickenham	won 36–6	1	11
11.10.91: USA	Twickenham	won 37–9	2	11
19.10.91: France	Paris	won 19–10	1	11
26.10.91: Scotland	Edinburgh	won 9–6		11
2.11.91: Australia	Twickenham	lost 6–12		11

1992

18.1.92: Scotland	Edinburgh	won 25–7	1	11
1.2.92: Ireland	Twickenham	won 38–9	1	11
15.2.92: France	Paris	won 31–13	1	11
7.3.92: Wales	Twickenham	won 24–0		11

Played 55   Won 33   Drawn 2   Lost 20   Tries 35

Other representative appearances for England

25.5.88:	Queensland B	Toowoomba	won 19–7	1	11
1.6.88:	South Australia President's XV	Adelaide	won 37–10	1	11
5.6.88:	New South Wales	Sydney	lost 12–23		11
7.7.91:	New South Wales	Sydney	lost 19–21	1	11
14.7.91:	Queensland	Brisbane	lost 14–20		14

Internationals for British Isles

16.4.86:	Rest of the World	Cardiff	lost 7–15	11
1.7.89:	Australia	Sydney	lost 12–30	11
8.7.89:	Australia	Brisbane	won 19–12	11
15.7.89:	Australia	Sydney	won 19–18	11
4.10.89:	France	Paris	won 29–27	11

Other British Isles appearances

10.6.89:	Western Australia	Perth	won 44–0	2	11
17.6.89:	Queensland	Brisbane	won 19–15		11
24.6.89:	New South Wales	Sydney	won 23–21		rep 11
27.6.89:	New South Wales B	Dubbo	won 39–19	2	11
4.7.89:	Australian Capital Territory	Queanbeyan	won 41–25		11

Representative matches

14.4.82:	England u-23 v England Students	Sheffield	lost 6–34		14
18.5.82:	England u-23 v Italy u-23	Treviso	won 15–0	1	11

20.5.82:	England u-23 v Italy B	Mantua	won 21–10	1	11
23.5.82:	England u-23 v Italy	Padua	lost 7–12		11
4.12.82:	England B v Ireland	Belfast	won 10–6		11
29.9.84:	England XV v President's XV	Twickenham	lost 10–27	1	11
9.4.86:	England u-23 v Spain	Twickenham	won 15–10		11
19.4.86:	Five Nations v Overseas Unions	Twickenham	lost 13–32		11
11.10.86:	England XV v Japan	Twickenham	won 39–12	1	11
15.5.88:	World XV v Australia	Sydney	lost 38–42		11
22.4.90:	Home Unions v Rest of Europe	Twickenham	won 43–18		11
29.9.90:	England XV v Barbarians	Twickenham	won 18–16		14
7.9.91:	England XV v USSR	Twickenham	won 53–0	2	14
21.9.91:	England XV v England Students	Cambridge	won 35–0	2	11

England colts

20.3.82:	French youth	Portsmouth	lost 3–16	11
3.4.82:	Welsh youth	Port Talbot	won 27–17	11

Barbarians

20.4.84:	Penarth	Penarth	won 32–21	2	11
23.4.84:	Swansea	Swansea	won 40–13	2	11
15.12.84:	Australians	Cardiff	lost 30–37	1	11
2.10.84:	Newport	Newport	lost 20–46	1	11
26.5.85:	Italy	Rome	won 23–15	1	11
14.9.85:	London Welsh	Twickenham	won 27–24	2	11
26.11.88:	Australians	Cardiff	lost 22–40		11
25.11.89:	New Zealanders	Twickenham	lost 10–21		11